'When it comes to handling complex ideas with clarity and accessibility, no one does it better than Peter Vardy. Here he gives meaning and purpose to being human, and shows how spiritual values transcend post-modern self-centredness and relativism. His argument is grounded in the Natural Law tradition, and affirms a common human nature which is radically authentic and ultimately accountable to Absolute Truth.'

John Saxbee, *Bishop of Lincoln*

'This is a timely and refreshing book. In the face of scientific reductionism Peter Vardy argues persuasively for a fuller, richer understanding of human nature. Emphasising man's capacity for transcendence and accountability to God, he contends for ultimate values over against the moral relativism of contemporary culture.'

Colin James, *Bishop of Winchester*

'Peter Vardy writes with exceptional clarity, first about ethical questions arising from developments in genetics and then about the more general issue of human fulfilment. His approach is based on the tradition of Natural Law, but the author also uses engagement with a broad range of philo-sophical and faith positions to present a robust defence of the concepts of truth and wisdom in the face of postmodernist criticism.'

John Polkinghorne, KBE, FRS

D1390021

Being Human

Fulfilling genetic and spiritual potential

PETER VARDY

DARTON·LONGMAN + TODD

First published in 2003 by
Darton, Longman and Todd Ltd
1 Spencer Court
140–142 Wandsworth High Street
London SW18 4JJ

ISBN 0 232 52455 6

A catalogue record for this book is available from the British Library.

Designed and produced by Sandie Boccacci
using QuarkXPress on an Apple PowerMac
Set in 10/13.25pt Palatino
Printed and bound in Great Britain by
The Bath Press, Bath

To Christa with love.
May you seek to fulfil your potential.

Contents

Acknowledgements

Many people have influenced me in writing this book. In particular colleagues, students and friends at Heythrop College, the specialist Theology and Philosophy College of the University of London, continually inspire and challenge by their lives, their example and the depth of their critical thinking.

For more than twenty years I have lectured on the theology and philosophy of Søren Kierkegaard whom Wittgenstein described as the greatest philosopher of the nineteenth century. Returning to his writings is always like coming back to a fresh pool of wisdom and depth. He has left a deep impression on everything I do, which these pages reflect.

I am particularly grateful for the criticisms and suggestions made by Julie Arliss of Richard Huish College, Taunton, without which this book would have been much the poorer. Virginia Hearn, my editor at DLT and a former Heythrop student, has been invaluable in providing insights and pointing out some of the errors.

The photograph on the cover was taken by my son, Luke, in the Namibian Desert.

PETER VARDY
Advent 2002

PART ONE

*The ancient Greek philosophers considered the
question 'How shall we live?' to be the most important
one of all. We are not only no nearer to finding an answer
but have forgotten the question.*

1

The Background to Ethical Impotence

What it means to become fully human is, today, far from clear. Many discussions concentrate on the human ability to manipulate the genome and the possibility of rectifying physical defects or enhancing physical characteristics. These issues will become an increasingly important part of the debate. However, there is a broader dimension to being human which is increasingly neglected. 'Spirituality' is a word much in vogue – included in the title of a book it will double sales ('Celtic spirituality' will triple them!) – but there is little clarity as to how this may relate to the quest to become fully human. This book is in two parts: in the first part the idea of a common human nature will be defended and the consequences for genetic engineering will be examined. The second part will focus more on what it means for a person to become a self, to fulfil his or her human potential in the face of widespread despair and meaninglessness. It will be argued that few today consider the question of 'Who am I?', and that failure to take this seriously underlies much of the futility perceived to lie beneath increasingly frenetic busyness and activity.

The Western world is, not to put too fine a point on it, in an ethical mess – and a mess of such proportions that most people don't even want to face up to it. The advance of science, cloning, genetic engineering and similar modern dilemmas provide challenges with which modern society does not know how to deal. There is no agreement on any set of values or ethical framework and, for many, life seems to be without any meaning except meanings derived from stories that are created and then lived out. The old certainties have gone, and society and individuals seem to be adrift on a sea of flotsam with no firm anchor points, no place from which ethical dilemmas can be judged. This book will argue that there is such a firm anchor point, in spite of the challenges by postmodernism and other forces to old certainties.

Individuals are faced with a bewildering array of dilemmas but, perhaps even more importantly, they are faced with challenges about meaning and purpose. The media dominates their short lives and creates wants that, even when satisfied, leave them feeling empty. In spite of labour-saving devices, most lives have never been busier, and time for reflection and relationships constantly declines. Society is fed with more and more information, children's lives are filled with more and more activity, and yet any meaning seems further away than ever.

For thousands of years God was held to underwrite claims to knowledge in all areas – not least in the field of morality. Most philosophers were religious believers and, whether they relied on introspection (such as Descartes who sought to doubt everything in order to arrive at the one thing he could be certain of – namely that he was a thinking thing) or sense experience (such as John Locke who believed that sense experience was the final arbiter of knowledge), nevertheless in the final analysis God underwrote all claims to knowledge. The world was there to be discovered and, whilst there may have been fierce intellectual arguments about what was and what was not true, there was little disagreement that there was truth to be sought and the philosopher's task was to find it.

The certainty given by a God-grounded universe did not last. Immanuel Kant began to unravel the widely accepted position when he argued that the phenomenal world, the world as it is experienced by human beings seen through the spectacles of space and time, was the only thing that could be known. The noumenal world, the 'real' world independent of the way it is experienced, was, Kant argued, in principle unknowable. This led to the situation in which human claims to knowledge are confined to the world of experience while the world as it actually is, independent of the way it is experienced, is deemed in principle inaccessible and unknowable. Kant was a firm believer in God, and his trust in God and the fairness of the universe underpinned much of his philosophy. He would have been horrified at the very suggestion that he was a contributor to the present ethical impotence. Nevertheless, once a divide was made between the world as it is experienced and the real world, the door was opened to the next move made by Hegel and then to Hegel's postmodern successors.

Hegel was influenced by Kant but he considered that his predecessor had made two fundamental mistakes. Firstly, he had failed to take into account any understanding of history and the development of ideas and, secondly, he had insisted on the existence of a real but inaccessible noumenal world independent of the world experienced by human beings.

Hegel rejected Kant's noumenal world. This seems a small point but, as with so many small points in the history of ideas, its impact was very great. Hegel argued that the real world is the world as we experience it but it is not just that our knowledge depends on our experiences – our experience conditions and in a sense creates the world which is real to us. There is no God in any conventional sense, instead 'Geist', or Absolute Spirit, becomes self-conscious in human beings, and Hegel's god is thus dependent on human beings.

For more than two thousand years Aristotle's 'principle of non-contradiction' had underpinned all philosophy. This holds that two contradictory statements cannot both be true – so 'p' and 'not-p' could not both be true at the same time. Hegel rejected this principle which for so long had underpinned traditional philosophy and argued that truth emerges through history and by means of the dialectical tensions between opposing positions. What appears at one level to be a contradiction may, at a higher level, be brought together in a synthesis. In essence truth becomes dependent on human beings: it emerges through the course of history and will change over time.

Hegel, effectively, took a significant move in rejecting the traditional idea of God as the creator and sustainer of the universe. He redefined what god meant in such a way that god largely depended on human beings. Human beings became the centre of the world of knowledge and a transcendent creator

God was no longer seen as relevant. As a result the underpinning of ethics by God was undermined, opening the door for it to become detached from any absolutes.

Karl Marx called Hegel's bluff. Hegel had got rid of Kant's real, noumenal world but still retained the idea of god as 'Geist' emerging through human rationality as part of the historical process. Hegel was a Christian and was seeking to defend a rational account of Christianity (albeit a heavily modified view of traditional Christianity) and of God. Marx saw that this attenuated view of God made religion irrelevant and so he faced up to the logical outcome of Hegel's position. Marx rejected all talk of God, placing humanity firmly in centre stage. Marx considered that human beings had to bring about social change in order to improve conditions here and now. There was no longer some utopian heaven after death which could justify placid acceptance of the status quo. Political action was necessary to assist the inevitable historical processes – Marx was influenced by Hegel's emphasis on progress through history – which would bring about the overthrow of the middle classes and the ownership of the means of production by the mass of ordinary people. This effectively meant by the government.

With humans now fully in centre stage, ethics became closely akin to sociology which was given intellectual licence to develop as the most fundamental discipline.

Dostoevsky's character Ivan Karamazov, in *The Brothers Karamazov*, rebelled against God on the grounds that the suffering of innocent children was too high a price to pay for any eventual salvation or state of bliss for a unique few. The novel brings home the consequences of a moral position in which, with the absence of God, 'everything is permitted'. Camus, in the twentieth century, was, in novels such as *The Plague* and *The Rebel*, to wrestle with how a rebellion against God in the name of humanity could within fifty years have resulted in millions of dead.

The pessimistic Schopenhauer regarded all life as being without meaning and futile, but it was Nietzsche who, in *Thus Spake Zarathustra*, pronounced God dead. Nietzsche contemplated a world free from the supposed tyranny of God and saw the ultimate goal of human beings as the production of the 'superman' who could transcend the categories of good and evil and who would create his (it was always male!) own morality free from the 'slave morality' (as he called it) of Christianity which, he said, had sapped the life out of the Roman empire and eventually destroyed it. Nietzsche died mad without realising the enormous significance of his writings or the impact they would have.

The slaughter of the First World War, when millions of young men from Europe, the old British Commonwealth and the United States died like cattle in an abattoir (in fact, in considerably worse conditions than cattle) for no clearly identifiable cause, undermined any idea of a social fabric in which God was in his heaven and all was right with the world. The old social order and the certainties that went with it were destroyed, cynicism began to set in, and social and religious structures were radically challenged.

Then in 1929, eleven years after the First World War ended, came the Great Depression which swept the developed world into a new form of crisis. The forces that brought about the depression seemed, to most people, to be inexplicable and affected rich and poor alike – but it was the poor, the workers, who inevitably suffered most. Just when hope had begun to be rekindled after the horror of the war and a new generation was being born and growing up, unemployment and social deprivation cut like a scythe through the countries of the Western world. Individuals saw no way out, caught as they were by forces beyond their understanding or control.

As the depression ended, so another war began. The Second World War, for some, seemed to restore order. Good was pitted against evil, right and wrong became more clearly delineated and, once more, a sense of community was rebuilt through the troubles of adversity. This feeling of community and of a perceived struggle against real evil seemed, for a time, to make the old distinctions between right and wrong meaningful once more.

The 1950s and 1960s were liberating for many. After the rationing and shortages of the Second World War, a new era of peace and prosperity in the Western world brought increased confidence. The old social conventions were undermined and by the end of the 1960s free love and drugs seemed, at least for some, to remove all the old taboos. The restrictions of the past were swept away and anything seemed possible.

Vietnam quickly brought disillusionment in the US and then, in a strange way, the world ran out of crises. Of course, people continued to be killed, wars continued to be fought and atrocities continued to be committed. Pol Pot's regime in Cambodia, Rwanda, the disintegration of Yugoslavia, Afghanistan, Chechnya, gang rape in wars throughout the world, starvation and natural disaster showed that suffering was alive and well and yet, in a sense, they became distanced from the affluent West – except through the media. For those in the United States, Europe, Australasia and the 'first world', life was good and seemed secure – more so with the death of communism and the old threat of an aggressive Soviet empire. The demolition of the Berlin Wall removed more than just a physical barrier and, driven by ecological and environmental concerns, the idea of the world becoming genuinely one began to surface.

The rioting French students of 1968 danced on the grave of the philosophic and theological past and truth came to seem a dirty word. Radical relativism became widely accepted and the Boston telephone book was placed on the reading list of the English Department of Harvard University as being of equal value to the works of Shakespeare. Out of the optimistic 1960s, fuelled by the Paris student riots in 1968, came a new intellectual movement that was to provide a devastating challenge to the old intellectual order and threaten to wipe it away. This was post-modernism which will be discussed late in the chapter.

All that was left was extreme liberalism and tolerance, which masked almost total relativism. This tolerance and relativism was a strength in that it challenged fundamentalism and the narrowly defined certainties of those who were convinced they had the truth and were determined to impose it on others. The idea that truth was relative to the community and even to the individual led to the tolerance of any opinion as being as valid and worthy of respect as any other. Once truth is accepted as relative, then the grounds for saying that some are right and others are wrong, that some are good and others are evil, disappear. This relativism seemed to place the final nail into the coffin of the old ethical and religious certainties.

The 'Twin Towers' attack in New York on September 11, 2001 was so devastating precisely because the suffering struck at the heart of Western democracy and the Western way of life. This way of life had seemed so secure that even wars could be fought by the United States and its allies, without allied casualties, from the air or by pilotless aircraft controlled from the ground. Prosperity kept increasing, unemployment was low, medical advances reduced suffering and, in many ways, an unrecognised golden age seemed to have dawned. Yet few would have described it in these terms as lurking under it all was a pervasive, unnoticed, unacknowledged yet widespread malaise. Psychological problems increased and the demand for counselling constantly rose as individuals sought to come to terms with the world in which they lived and yet from which they often felt alienated. The Twin Towers attacks also showed that the apparent security of the West was an illusion and, as the threat of terrorist attacks grows ever wider, this apparent security is likely to be seen to be increasingly illusory.

The world is left with greater poverty and greater wealth, with greater technology and greater inequality, than at any time in history. Most of the developed nations have great prosperity, albeit masking tremendous and rising wealth gaps between the very rich and the poor. There is a perceived lack of almost all meaning combined with a small but rising tide of religious fundamentalism which some feel provides a bedrock of certainty in an uncertain age.

Increasingly, human beings are like headless chickens running around the farmyard with great rapidity, not knowing where they are or where they are going and yet still convinced that all is well despite being possessed of a suppressed feeling that the situation is much more serious than it appears to be. Many ethical dilemmas face individuals and societies and these seem so complex and multi-faceted that people have no way of grappling with them. The world seems to be caught in the grip of anonymous forces that few understand, let alone control:

- Conflicts become increasingly complex and deciding whether a war is just or not has become almost impossible.
- The motivations driving politicians concerned with re-election are increasingly complex and hard to judge. An unacknowledged utilitarian approach pervades most democracies but there is little analysis of the consequences for those excluded from the benefits of economic success.
- Globalisation means that jobs are lost in the West and transferred to the third world whilst, on the other hand, the West protects certain of its industries and prevents the third world competing. There is unprecedented wealth coupled with massive poverty extending across entire regions (such as sub-Saharan Africa).
- Business ethics are meant to be taken seriously but huge frauds are perpetrated which destroy some of the largest companies in the world.
- Medical ethics become increasingly complex and resolving the issues appears to be increasingly impossible.
- Increased concern for the safety of children and worries about paedophilia mean that children are never left alone. They are accompanied almost everywhere and the opportunity to play and explore unaccompanied by adults has almost disappeared.
- The power of television grows ever greater, imparting values which are incredibly powerful but not understood. Most parents are unable to challenge them since the media influences them as much as their children.
- The Internet links people together and provides information in a way unimagined in the past, yet there is greater social isolation and, perhaps, less wisdom than ever.
- Religion is seen to be increasingly irrelevant by many and yet the greatest growth in the religious area is by fundamentalist groups which increasingly pervade even old established churches and religions.*

---

* *What is Truth* by Peter Vardy (Alresford, John Hunt Publishing, 2003) explores these issues in more depth and attempts to chart a middle way between fundamentalism and postmodernism.

There is no single cause of these difficulties, but one contributory factor is the complexity of postmodernism and this needs to be understood before any attempt can be made to formulate a way forward.

Postmodernism

There is no one thing that postmodernism is. To this extent, post-modernism is extremely postmodern. It resists being captured by any simple definition and any definition will always be inadequate. Consequently, 'postmodernism' is a word that is in common currency but few people know what it means or understand its implications. Since there is no one definition of postmodernism, any attempt at an explanation will always be inadequate and deemed to be superficial by those with greater knowledge and insight.

In my book *What is Truth* I used the following image. Imagine you are at sea in a raging storm. You seek for a place of safety, some rock to cling to, some refuge where you can escape the ravages of the fierce currents which toss you hither and thither. Philosophers have sought for such a place of security for three thousand years – they have sought Truth (with a capital 'T') or to arrive at ultimate meaning and thus to be secure from change. The hymn 'Abide with Me' by H. F. Lyte expresses this well:

> Change and decay in all around I see
> Oh thou who changest not, abide with me.

Plato saw the whole world as changing and claimed that the philosopher must seek refuge from this shadow world of change in the unchanging, fixed reality of the Forms of the Good, the Beautiful, the True and the Just. These perfect ideas, existing beyond time and space, found their pale reflections in our world and every instance of goodness, beauty, truth and justice in some way reflected these perfect and unchanging Ideas or Forms. They were the rocks that provided security. With the advent of Christianity, God was seen as providing similar security – a fixed point of meaning, truth and value in an unstable world.

Postmodernism denies that there are any such rocks of certainty. It calls to human beings in the raging sea to abandon the search for rocks, to 'go with the flow' and simply to seek to understand where they are. There are no rocks. Humans are in water-world – the fixed landmarks have all gone. All is flux, all is change, and all depends on perspective.

Just as there is no clear definition of what postmodernism is, there is no single moment when it began. To the postmodern philosopher, context and perspective are everything and the reality humans talk about and inhabit is simply one that they construct. It is a constantly changing reality, a virtual world with no fixed point. Postmodernism involves a rejection of any attempt to make sense of the world as any sense will depend on what the observer reads into the world. There is no meaning, no truth, no sense to be discovered.

There is no absolute meaning, whether in life, religion or morality or even the text of a book – since the way that a text is interpreted will depend on the culture within which it is read. Similarly, the very idea that there is a 'right' reading of a book or that one can seek to establish the 'correct' understanding of a text (whether the Bible, the Qu'ran, Shakespeare or a novel) is, for the postmodernist, simply nonsense which fails to take into account that it is the reaction of the reader to the text which is vital. The Torah, Bible, Qu'ran or any other holy book is, therefore, denied any privileged status.

Postmodernism rejects any meta-narrative – any overarching, 'true' picture of the world. Once truth is truly abandoned, then there really is no truth to be sought; people must be content with truth that is simply dependent on perspective.

There are no absolutes, no rocks of certainty on which one can stand firm outside the constant sea of change. All humans are adrift in these tossing and raging waters and reality is merely their own perspective. To talk of raging waters is, in fact, to go back a long way in the history of philosophy – to Heraclitus who maintained the very postmodern position that everything is subject to change and truth is something we create.

Postmodernism claims that the most we can achieve, by great effort, is to try to understand another's perspective whilst recognising that he or she is also immersed in the constant waters of change. His or her perspective is no better or worse than ours. The search for certainty or for any rock to cling to is folly. Truth (at least with a capital 'T'), meaning and values have become dirty words, words used only by those who, having failed to appreciate the human condition, remain embedded in a world view which is considered discredited. As Nietzsche puts it: 'facts are precisely what there is not, only interpretations.'[*]

This represents a radical shift in perspective which, even today, most ordinary people would not accept. Postmodernists tend to assume that their position is correct and often lack patience in arguing for it against what they perceive as the more naïve ordinary view that there are some absolute truths. Many post-modernists appear to see themselves in a position of superiority over more naïve mortals who do not accept their position and sometimes seem disinclined to argue for it. It is as if once a person has seen that the earth goes round the sun and that the sun is a relatively unimportant planet in a minor galaxy, he will have little to say to a friend who still considers that the world is flat and that the sun goes round the earth. The shift in perspective is so great that communication becomes almost impossible and the only hope may be to try to persuade the friend to open his or her mind and to see the situation in a new way. So it is with post-modernists and those whom they see as being still obsessed by the old ideas of metaphysics and a search for meaning and truth. They share a mutual incomprehension which, for the post-modernist, will only be overcome as those who still think in these 'outmoded' ways expand their vision, to come out of the trenches formed by their mind and see the world in a broader perspective. Argument will not achieve the shift in perspective. What is needed is for these people to stop closing their minds, to be open to new possibilities and to be able to live on the sea of uncertainty with no fixed marks and where nothing abides or endures. Young people today, however, need no convincing of the truth of post-modernism – they are fed a postmodernist diet from birth and any alternative seems incomprehensible.

---

[*] *The Will to Power*, tr. Kaufmann (New York, Random House, 1987), p. 481.

Postmodernism has little time for the old European cultural ideas based on Christian values. They are seen as male-dominated and to have been used as a means of suppression, particularly of women and indigenous peoples. When the European colonial powers spread round the world, they imposed their own values and religion by force of arms. Thus, young children in Africa sang nineteenth-century English hymns which included lines about good King Wenceslas wading through the snow or the need to preach the gospel to the poor, benighted heathen, and were educated into Western images and Western means of measuring success. Local culture was thereby destroyed or totally undermined. Resistance to the colonial imposition was seen as resistance to progress and to all things modern, right and good. To the postmodernist, there were no redeeming features of colonialism – it was an exercise in power, the imposition of one set of beliefs and values on another. Once one accepts that there is no meaning, no ultimates, then any such imposition is merely an exercise in power. Professor Quirrell in the first Harry Potter volume *The Philosopher's Stone*,* expresses this when he says: 'There is no right and wrong, there is only power and those with the will to use it.'

Western imperialism and 'values' have been responsible for slavery, oppression and the marginalisation of women. It is self-evident that the history of the world appears to have been written from a male perspective and it is only recently that feminist voices have begun to surface. Postmodernists are highly critical of the old order which they see as wanting to retain its power through the imposition of its values on everyone else. The dominance of those with power and those who control the media is undeniable – as, for instance, the selling power of the logos of Coca Cola and McDonald's clearly demonstrate. The products of such high-profile companies have become the objects of desire and of value in many countries around the world. Coca Cola is the most widely recognised name and symbol in the world and poor young people in Africa will spend a significant amount of their income on consuming, and therefore

---

* London, Bloomsbury Children's Books, 1999.

identifying with, the image that Coca Cola evokes. McDonald's can be found in almost every country in the world and, again, in many countries represents something to aspire to. Coca Cola's advertisement claiming that 'It's the real thing' is viewed by postmodernists with some irony as a good example of an exercise in power.

Since truth in any absolute sense has disappeared, no one religious perspective is any longer seen as true. Belief in ancestral spirits, voodoo, atheism, witchcraft, Christianity and Sikhism are regarded by many to have as much value as each other. Missionary activity is discredited as an exercise in power bringing about the destruction of culture. Tolerance, therefore, becomes the new god and any who do not accept this new creed are to be opposed and rejected.

The extending influence of the Western media, whether CNN or News International, is considered by postmodernists to represent power in action. Seldom, it is claimed, do those in the West see or realise the injustice perpetrated by the World Bank, GATT, world trade organisations and the like or, for instance, the tremendous damage to local people done by so-called 'development projects' such as new dams, chemical works or the like. The world is seen through a single set of spectacles: a partial, biased and inadequate view of what is happening, which fails to respect the 'others', those who are different, and the way that they are oppressed. It is very easy, if one assumes that one's own values are 'right', to consider that all those who accept these values are right as well. This is exactly what postmodernism rejects. If all perspectives are of equal value, then what is needed is respect and understanding for the 'other', for the stranger, the alien – not to see him or her only through our own eyes. There are no rights or wrongs – just alternative perspectives. The status quo is maintained by the power of the media.

The Hebrew Scriptures recognised an uncompromising duty to care for and preserve the stranger – no matter what the cost. But the stranger is precisely the one who is different, the one who is alien. Today many people force strangers to become as 'we' are before they will recognise them and 'we' even enter their societies and demand (through the media, advertising and the world economic order) that the population of the world accept 'our' values and suppress or reject their own. This, post-modernists claim, is one more exercise in power and is fundamentally unjust.

The same rejection of the use of imposed ideas would, of course, apply to any alternative system, for instance, Islam, which claimed that it had the 'right' answer and which attempted to impose its beliefs. There are strong echoes of anarchism (a necessary result of multiple claims to truth) within postmodernism which resists any authority and any imposition of a system or rules although, strangely by its own criteria, it has its own authors, its own heroes and heroines who are elevated to a status which, on their own account, none should enjoy. Any philosophic, religious or scientific framework needs to be abandoned or at least treated with the gravest suspicion.

The postmodern individual lives in a world of openness and uncertainty. This is apparently liberating and invigorating as there are no boundaries, nothing that cannot be challenged, and it can lead to great creativity. It is exactly where Western society seemed to have arrived at in the late 1960s. Everyone is free, everyone is liberated from the old values. True freedom has arrived and everyone can make their own truth and their own reality.

The trouble is that this freedom, so hard won, has turned to dust. Many now seek precisely what they have supposedly out-grown. Meaninglessness surrounds the lives of many in the West and despair lurks in quiet moments. Religious fundamentalism is on the increase as people yearn for the old certainties. They have arrived at where they thought they wanted to be and discovered that it is exactly where they do not want to be. Yet now they have arrived in the new utopia, the path back seems blocked. It is this that leads to the rise of cults, to extreme political forces and allegiance to power figures who proclaim the certainty that many yearn for and which is now lost. With no agreed standards rhetoric, media power and sexual power can all affect the minds of a nation as there is no longer an ability or willingness to consider the distinction between good and evil.

The Implications for Ethics

The ethical implications of these developments have been cata-strophic as the notion of an agreed ethical framework by reference to which moral judgements may be made has been lost. Such a framework, it will later be argued, should never be decisive in making ethical decisions but in its absence ethical questions barely arise. This lack of ground is concealed by a general liberal sympathy for 'human rights' and the idea of democracy and freedom. On closer examination, however, there are few agreed human rights and when examined they come close to being an attempt by the West to impose their own standards on radically different cultures. Democracy, for all its strengths, depends largely on marketing and media promotion. The figures in the United States for the amount of money spent to secure election both at local, senate and presidential elections provide clear evidence for this. With success in elections gener-ally depending on an ability to outspend the competition, democracy becomes a word used to describe the financial elite maintaining power on their own terms. The concentration of media power into a few hands reinforces this with the pro-prietors of the major media outlets imposing their own views on the electorate.

In the US the power of the military/industrial and farming lobbies prevents the publication of stories which might be detri-mental to their interests, such as those that are critical of certain forms of armaments (for instance, cluster bombs) or those that are critical of friends of the US (such as the State of Israel), or that run counter to powerful interests (such as the genetic engineer-ing of plants). In spite of this, Americans prize themselves on living in 'the land of the free' – yet this land demands conformi-ty on a scale which comes close to rivalling that of communism at the height of its powers. After the September 11, 2001 attacks on the Twin Tower, some philosophers who questioned US policy suggesting it might have given rise to the attacks, were pilloried, marginalised, silenced and faced death threats. This insistence on conformity to the 'American way' leaves little scope for genuine ethical reflection.

Of course, there are those who take moral stands, but these stands often represent power-plays by groups with vested interests. In the US the anti-abortion lobby is closely associated with the Moral Majority which has clear political ambitions. The same groups who campaign so fiercely on some issues are silent on others where their own vested interests come into play – for instance, on issues of social justice, the rights of women, arms or gun control, or globalisation.

A new approach to ethics is needed which can recognise the claims of postmodernism and can deal with the challenges of the twenty-first century. The challenge posed by genetic engineering is a good example of an ethical challenge that is still not fully understood and this can provide a litmus test for the success of any proposed new ethical approach.

2

A Test Case –
The Challenge of
Genetic Engineering

There is no easy response to the postmodern challenge, particularly when it is coupled with the complexity of the many ethical dilemmas with which society is faced. One particular new moral problem can provide a helpful litmus test for any attempt at a successful solution to the ethical difficulties human beings now face, and that is the dilemmas posed by genetic engineering.

The past fifty years has been a time of unprecedented breakthroughs:

- 1952: First calf produced using frozen semen
- 1953: Frozen sperm used for human artificial insemination
- 1967: First human heart transplanted
- 1970: Mouse embryos cloned
- 1973: First calf produced from frozen embryos
- 1979: First sheep embryos cloned
- 1980: Nobel sperm bank founded
- 1983: Baby born using father's sperm and donor egg
- 1984: Girl born from frozen embryo. Baboon's heart transplanted into child
- 1990: Human genome project starts
- 1993: Human embryos cloned
- 1997: First sheep cloned
- 1998: Stem cells isolated
- 2000: Human genome mapped. This may well be the most significant development of the last hundred years and its consequences are still only dimly appreciated.

The pace of change in genetics and medicine in this period has been greater than in the past 2000 years.

James Watson shared with Francis Crick the Nobel prize for the discovery of the DNA double helix in 1953. Their research gave rise to the whole field of genetics and, in 2000, the whole of the human genome was mapped for the first time. In April 2001 James Watson launched a campaign to rid society of genetic defects by the genetic engineering of human embryos: 'I strongly favour controlling our children's genetic destinies. Working intelligently and wisely to see that good genes dominate as many lives as possible is the truly moral way for us to proceed.'*

Within the next fifteen to fifty years it now seems inevitable that, for the more wealthy members of Western society, 'Gen-Rich' children will become the norm. 'Gen-rich' children are those whose genetic profile has been enhanced or defects eliminated by using germ line genetic engineering. Germ line gene therapy involves the insertion of normal genes into fertilised eggs in an attempt to create a genetic change which can be transmitted to an organism's offspring (for example, to correct for a defective genetic trait leading to deformity or disease). If a change is introduced via germ line gene therapy then this change will be present in the offspring from birth in every cell in the body. This generally involves using the retrovirus vector, which passes on its own genes to cells with which it makes contact, to make alterations either to individual genes or strings of genes in order either to eliminate defects or to develop certain characteristics (which are likely to include hair and eye colour, body shape, intelligence, and others). Increasingly, those choosing to have 'naturals' (i.e. children resulting from conventional sexual activity with a partner where the genetic profile of the resulting child depends on the accident of which of 2 million of the male's sperm reaches its target first and which of the mother's 500,000 eggs happens to ripen and descend into the Fallopian tube in the particular month in question) will become progressively socially marginalised. Many believe that there will be initial resistance to

---

* All the quotations from James Watson are taken from an article published in *The Independent* on 16 April 2001.

this trend, as there has always been resistance to new discoveries and developments, but a number of factors will combine to make the acceptability of gen-rich children inexorable.

Governments throughout the Western world are faced with continually greater demands for health care provision. In North America, Europe, Australasia, Japan, Singapore and the remaining countries of the 'first world' the new developments in medical technology enable people to live longer, healthier lives – but the economic costs are great. The people of almost all democracies want lower taxes and, therefore, legislators are caught in a pincer movement. On the one hand their election depends on them promising to reduce, or at least not to increase, taxes and, on the other hand, the demands for medical costs rise inexorably. Germ line genetic engineering should enable costs to be reduced by eliminating diseases and deformities at the embryo stage – thus saving the State huge amounts of money. The ability to rid children of Down's syndrome, Hutchinson's disease, certain cancers, cystic fibrosis and many other diseases through genetic engineering at the foetal stage will transform medicine and, with it, the whole basis of medical care. Preventative medicine has for long been considered desirable but in the West there will soon be within reach the ability to prevent a very wide range of diseases by genetic engineering to ensure that children are born without the genetic defects that will give rise to illnesses later in life.

Genetic testing is now widely available. It is used, for instance, to predict diseases and also to settle paternity suits. As a matter of routine police forces now employ genetic testing to identify criminals and support grows for national databases which can be accessed to determine who committed crimes. It is almost impossible to walk into a room without leaving genetic traces behind and these traces can provide well-nigh conclusive evidence of a person's presence. Genetic information on all individuals will soon be part of the data accumulated by the State. Obviously this information will be controlled and people will be reassured that it will not be released without their permission but in practice this is not a safeguard. Once this information is available it will be impossible to stop insurance companies and potential employers requiring access. If an individual refuses to give permission for this access to be given, this will in itself be enough for an insurer to refuse insurance cover or for a company to refuse to employ someone. The refusal of access will, in itself, come to be seen as grounds for suspicion and, at the very least, for rigorous further investigation. The desirability of a good genetic profile for children will, therefore, increase.

As genetic profiling becomes more precise and as genetic information disseminates more widely, those children with indifferent genetic profiles will find it increasingly difficult to obtain employment or insurance. The film *Gattaca* portrays this well – a new apartheid is almost certain to arise based not on colour, sex, age, race or religion but on genetic profile. It seems probable that dyslexia and dyscalculia are genetic and it should be possible to determine, at birth or before, whether these defects are present – this may well have an effect on school admissions policies.

Parents always want what is best for their unborn children. If asked whether they would prefer a boy or a girl, most will reply that they are not worried provided it is healthy. Most potential parents also carry a fear, however unfounded this may be, that their new baby may be in some way defective. Genetic engineering will enable parents to ensure that defects are eliminated and, thus, to have the assurance that their baby will carry no significant genetic problems into their later life.

To choose to breed 'naturals' when the 'gen-rich' option is available is likely to become increasingly unacceptable. Today a woman who smokes, takes drugs or drinks – beyond in moderation – during pregnancy will be generally criticised and possibly condemned by her friends and by society since such behaviour harms the baby. Some women have been arrested by so-called 'pregnancy police' because they took substances such as cocaine which were considered harmful to their unborn children and given comparatively long prison sentences. The condemnation of, for instance, smoking when pregnant is new – thirty years ago this would hardly have been questioned. Similarly, once it is possible to rid children of the tendency to suffer disease or inherited defects at the foetal stage, then any mother who refuses to take the necessary steps is, in the near future, likely to be socially condemned. It is one thing to have a Down's syndrome child when this is considered 'an act of God' but quite another to choose to have a Down's child when, with a simple procedure, this child could have been born normal.

When these factors are combined both with government initiatives to ensure women have healthy babies and with the power of advertising from the companies that have patents over the new technology, the social acceptability of gen-rich children is almost assured.

Watson says: 'To my knowledge, not one illness, much less fatality, has been caused by a genetically manipulated organism.' Of those, therefore, that say all genetic engineering should be abandoned from fear of unknown consequences in the future, he is simply dismissive: 'Never postpone experiments that have clearly defined future benefits for fear of dangers that cannot be quantified.' Watson is claiming here that the benefits of ensuring our children have good gene profiles are so strong that any unquantifiable potential risks should be ignored or, if they arise, should be capable of being dealt with by science.

If germ line genetic engineering and embryo research are not allowed, then all scientific advance may be ruled out for fear of the unknown and the huge potential health and cost benefits that may be possible (through lower medical costs) will not be achieved. As Watson says: '... never put off something useful for fear of evil that may never arrive. We can react rationally only to real, not hypothetical, risks ... Working intelligently and wisely to see that good genes dominate as many lives as possible is the truly moral way to proceed.'

James Watson's campaign is still in its infancy, but companies are now allowed to patent gene sequences and all the legislation is now in place to enable gen-rich children to be selected. Given the reasons above, it seems likely that only religious funda-mentalists will hold out against the new technology. Once the benefits are explained and the new techniques are actively promoted, then the benefits of the technology will be accepted by most people as being both in the best interests of the present and future generations.

Scientists today are held with the respect once reserved for priests. As religion has become a minority activity so priests have become marginalised. Priests, even of a single denomination, no longer speak with a single voice, and too many cases of child abuse or homosexual and heterosexual relationships by so-called celibate priests have been documented in the newspapers for their views any longer to hold the sway that they once did. Instead, scientists are given the respect and authority priests once enjoyed. They are held to hold the key to health and long life in a similar way to which priests once held the keys to heaven. Scientists base their findings on empirical evidence and if they reassure people that genetic engineering can provide the promise of healthy, defect-free children as well as the cure to many conditions that are presently considered incurable, the attractions of these techniques will be very great and are likely to sweep away all opposition.

The Implications for Ethics

Modern society today has almost no ethical framework in which to consider the issues raised by genetic engineering. Churches either fall silent or utter general condemnations which many do not understand or which are perceived to be behind the current technological developments as well as being based on ethical systems developed more than 2000 years ago. For those outside the most faithful adherents of particular belief systems, the pronouncements of religious groups do not seem to have a convincing intellectual basis in the postmodern world. Television programmes and soap operas set out moral dilemmas which show the inadequacy of old, simplistic rules but offer no clear way forward. Many young people grow up in a moral vacuum in which these issues are not even addressed and their parents feel uniquely disabled in suggesting ways forward.

This book will attempt to address the problem of relativism and a denial of truth in ethics or religion that postmodernism proposes. It will also attempt to set out a new way forward, albeit a way rooted in the past, which can deal with the complexities of genetic engineering as this provides a litmus test for any successful approach to ethics in today's world. The book is in two parts – and the significance of these two parts will become clear later.

3

Being Human

There is no longer any agreed system of ethics, no way of tackling the many ethical dilemmas with which the contemporary world confronts us. Many people have no clear centre to their lives – nothing to give their lives clear meaning and direction. Yet the ethical dilemmas become more grave and difficult all the time. There is little space in people's lives for stillness or for personal reflection. As we have seen, two positions are in tension:

1. Conformity to contemporary society and to the ideas of the value setters who largely determine the values of society through the media is the norm. A postmodern tolerance and respect for every alternative view rules.
2. Those who try to resist this tide by holding on to certainties which they proclaim with increasing stridency end up talking largely to themselves and those already converted to their own narrow views.

The suspicion of absolutes which cannot be justified seems to lead inevitably to relativism. Where, then, can one look for a basis for ethical reflection in a postmodern, post-Christian world? Don Cupitt's book *The Sea of Faith** drew on the poem 'Dover Beach' by Matthew Arnold which saw faith as a dwindling sea, receding from the shore line where once it was dominant:

---

* *The Sea of Faith* (London, SCM Press, 1994) was the first book to clearly present the case for religious anti-realism which sees God reality as something that is constructed by human beings.

The Sea of Faith
Was once, too, at the full, and round earth's shore
Lay like the folds of a bright girdle furled.
But now I only hear
Its melancholy, long, withdrawing roar,
Retreating, to the breath
Of the night-wind, down the vast edges drear
And naked shingles of the world.

The Sea of Faith movement and anti-realists consider all religious and ethical truth claims to be constructs created by the communities which adhere to them. This merely reinforces the postmodern agenda which sees truth as a human construct. Anti-realists will still talk of claims to truth in ethics, but the truths will be contained within different communities and systems where they have gradually developed and become accepted.

This book will argue that, in spite of all the challenges to old religious certainties, there is still a firm anchor point for the ethical debate. Indeed, it is a very old anchor point having been first developed by Aristotle, then affirmed and adopted in the Western Christian tradition culminating in the work of St Thomas Aquinas in the thirteenth century, confirmed as central to Catholic ethics at the Council of Trent and still affirmed, at least in principle although not so much in practice, by the modern Catholic Church. However, by virtue of the fact that it is not distinctively Christian but is based on reason, it is accessible to people of all faiths, or none. The approach is grounded on what it is to be a human being.

Greek philosophy sought to answer the question 'How should we live?' and did so by reference to our common humanity. Traditional Christian ethics, other than in the more evangelical Protestant churches, has been centred on the claim that all human beings share a common human nature and that it is possible to work out what this nature is by using reason alone. This insight came from Aristotle who argued that every animal and plant had a distinct nature which could be determined by studying the animal or plant in question. Wombats, seagulls and dandelions have, respectively, a wombat, seagull and dandelion nature and, therefore, in order to understand these natures one needs to study wombats, seagulls and dandelions.

The fact that his approach was based on empirical observation of the object of study, has resulted in Aristotle being considered the first Western scientist. For Aristotle, every living thing had a soul or psyche – but this was very different from soul in the sense used by Plato, who as a dualist considered the soul as a separate substance, distinct from the human body in which it was contained. Aristotle considered that to talk of 'soul' was not to talk of a separate 'something' existing within the human body which could separate on death, but 'soul' or 'psyche' was, rather, the principal of the organisation of living things – it was what made a dandelion a dandelion, a wombat a wombat or a human being a human being. 'Soul', the principle of the organisation of living things, therefore belonged to every living thing from a flower to an oak tree, from a slug to a kangaroo and from an ape to a human being. All animals or plants are made up of matter, but this matter needs to be organised to make the thing what it is and this organisation is provided by the form or soul of a thing. This led to the view that all human beings, because they are human beings, share a common human nature. Because human beings are human, they all share a single human nature represented by the common soul or principle which governs their organisation.

The soul of an oak tree is in an acorn – in other words, the principle of organisation which makes an oak tree what it is, is found in the little acorn. This does not mean, of course, that an acorn *is* an oak tree, nevertheless they share the same nature. There are close links here with modern ideas of genetics. The acorn has the potential to grow into an oak tree – if its potential is actualised then the acorn will become that which it was intended to become by its nature, namely an oak tree. It will never become a flower or a beech tree. Three principles, then, are vital to Aristotle:

1. To talk of soul is to talk of the principle that governs living things of a particular type.
2. This principle can be defined in terms of the potential of the thing to become what it is intended to be.

3. Human beings share a common human nature and have the potential to develop into full human beings.

In the case of a human, this can be expressed as follows:
1. A zygote is not the same as a foetus but it has the potential to become a foetus.
2. A foetus is not the same as a baby but it has the potential to become a baby.
3. The baby is not the same as a young child, but has the potential to become a young child.
4. A child is not the same as a teenager, but has the potential to become a teenager.
5. A teenager is not the same as an adult but has the potential to become an adult.

In fact, of course, this can be simplified by saying that zygote, embryo, foetus, baby, child and teenager all share the potential to become an adult. As they grow, their potential is realised but the potential is there in the zygote as much as it is in the teenager. This is central to Aristotle's understanding not just of human beings but of all living things – each living thing has its own nature and at each stage it has the potential to develop fully into whatever the thing is.

However, Aristotle's analysis did not stop there. Take the case of a butterfly. A butterfly's egg has the potential to become a caterpillar, the caterpillar to become a butterfly. But even when egg and caterpillar have actualised their potential and become a butterfly, this is not the end. The butterfly may be dormant – in this case the butterfly has potentialities (flying, moving, mating) that it is not actualising. Only once the adult butterfly is active, using its potential to the full, does it become fully what it is intended to be. Crucial, therefore, to understanding what it is to be a butterfly (or anything else) is to understand what its potential is. This is not as obvious as it appears.

Aristotle considered that every living thing – plants, animals and human beings – have the potential to reproduce. Of course, this potential is actualised in different ways by different species. Some give birth, some lay eggs; some reproduce singly, others multiply; for some sexual reproduction involves two sexes, some are hermaphrodites and some reproduce simply by division – however, they all reproduce in ways that are appropriate to their particular species. If one wants to work out what the potentialities of any living organism are (and only living organisms have these potentialities), then this involves studying these organisms to work out what they are – in other words, they have to be studied to determine their nature.

The nature of a thing will be defined in terms of what it is and what it has the potential to be. So, an acorn is a seed of a particular size, type, colour, etc., and it has the potential to become an oak tree. This oak tree has the potential to grow and in due course to reproduce. It has the potential to be a home for birds and countless varieties of insects and other creatures. There is, naturally, no guarantee that any potential will be actualised. A squirrel may eat the acorn and then the acorn's potentialities are at an end. The acorn no longer exists. Similarly, a scientist may collect the acorn and irradiate it so that it is no longer capable of growing. In this case, also, the potentialities of the acorn are at an end and, for Aristotle, it is no longer an acorn. Of course, it may still look like an acorn, but since its potentialities have been destroyed it is no longer an acorn. Someone may reply to this, 'Of course it is still an acorn. Look at it. It still looks like an acorn and if you ask anyone what it is then they will say it is an acorn.' Appearances, however, can be deceptive. The fact that a thing looks as though it is of a particular kind does not mean that it is. A clever model of an acorn made out of Plasticine might deceive many into thinking that it was, indeed, an acorn – but they would be mistaken. Certainly it looks like an acorn, but it isn't. Similarly, an irradiated acorn looks like an acorn, but it is no longer an acorn. Its potentialities are at an end and in a very real sense it is dead – as dead as if the squirrel had eaten it.

An ethical approach committed to the view that what is crucial in human development is 'to become fully human', to become what we are fully capable of becoming, obviously starts with a key premise that can and will be rejected by many at the outset. This is the claim that there is something called a human nature which all human beings share. Postmodernism would reject this totally, and this challenge has to be recognised and answered. Postmodernists would hold that human nature is not fixed or given but is a construct, just as all claims to truth are constructs. What it is to be human is not something that is discovered by careful enquiry, instead it is something that is created by human beings and will vary depending on who is doing the creating. What it is to be human will, according to postmodern perspectives, be defined and understood differently by a middle-class, middle-aged, heterosexual male than by a working-class, Afro-American, female transsexual. There are an infinite number of human natures depending on the many different factors that affect human beings, including race, age, economic circum-stances, gender and sexual orientation. The attempt to argue for or impose a single understanding of what it is to be human is an attempt, postmodernists will assert, to impose an understanding which everyone is meant to accept. This, they will contend, is what Christianity has always done, using the coercive power of the media, culture, education and the Church to marginalise and oppress women, homosexuals, the poor and the different. There is considerable strength to this view and it needs to be taken seriously. The postmodern view just outlined which recognises the differences between human beings, is valid. The failure of Christian moral theology in the Middle Ages to grapple with this and other questions resulted, to give just one example, in the differences between male and female human beings being given the simplistic explanation that a female was a defective male (interestingly, this was an idea that Freud was also to take seriously). However, it is possible, and indeed essential, to talk of a common human nature in a more developed sense than that adopted in the Middle Ages. To do so, it is necessary to bring together a number of contemporary disciplines including philosophy, theology, psychology, sociology and anthropology.

One of the reasons why the Christian Church accepted Aristotle's ideas was that they seemed to confirm the biblical view that human beings were created by God with a distinct nature. If this nature was God-given, then it made sense to claim that human beings had an obligation to fulfil it. However, Aristotle did not think in these terms. Aristotle's god was the unmoved mover who did not create or sustain the universe, or have any interest in it. God, for Aristotle, contemplated god's self and was, therefore, supremely happy. Matter was eternal and was not created. Because of the irrelevance of god to Aristotle's model, there is no reason why an atheist, a humanist or a Buddhist, who do not believe in the existence of God, could not accept that humans share a common human nature.

Five arguments can be given to justify this claim against those who argue that there is no such thing as a human nature:

1. Although there are undoubtedly differences between human beings, such as gender, sexuality, intelligence, socio-economic grouping and the like, as well as differences of colour, hair type, appearance, height, etc., nevertheless it remains the case that a distinct human nature exists which is not a construct. It is true in an absolute sense that human beings have two eyes, two ears, a nose, mouth, lungs, heart, kidneys, are carbon based yet are substantially made from water, stand upright on two feet, have adaptable thumbs which make it possible to manipulate tools and many, many other common characteristics. Of course, one can still be human and be missing some of these features but they nevertheless constitute what it is to be human. These are facts about what it is to be human that are discovered and are not made up. Of course human beings differ (every person's fingerprint is different and every person's DNA is unique), yet there is a unity underlying the difference.

2. International law is based on the claim that there is a single human nature. It is on this assumption that the whole idea of 'crimes against humanity' rests. At the Nuremburg trials after the Second World War, senior Nazis were put on trial for 'crimes against humanity'. Some Nazis rejected the basic premise that such crimes existed – instead they maintained that Nuremburg was simply a case of the victor's morality being allowed to judge the vanquished. Morality, they claimed, was relative to culture – it was based on power and the decisions of those who exercise this power. Hitler's government had been democratically elected and they were obeying laws and orders given by an internationally recognised government. This was an important defence which, if

proved valid, would have caused the case to collapse. However, this claim was dismissed, and ever since that time, international legal bodies have recognised that crimes against humanity do indeed occur: they are crimes not because they go against any particular set of laws but because they violate basic, common human nature. It is on the basis of the existence of this common human nature that war crimes trials take place in The Hague, and very few people would disagree that the act of genocide represents a crime against human nature.

3. The claim that all human beings share an innate, common human nature is the basis on which human rights discussions are built. Human rights, it is held, are not conferred, they are innate. These rights do not depend on any government but are intrinsic: they cannot be taken away. This is the basis of the human rights declarations of France, the US and the United Nations. It is true, of course, that there are disagreements as to what these rights are – do they, for instance, include the right to work, to leisure and to freedom of political expression? Despite the fact that not all governments agree about their definition, however, all governments, irrespective of political ideology, do agree that there are such rights (every government has signed the UN Declaration of Human Rights even if there are some differences of interpretation). It is because of the innate nature of these rights that there is such heavy criticism when any government tries to ignore them or take them away – if rights were conferred, then the Nazi government could have been justified in deciding to remove them from Jews, homosexuals or those who were handicapped. If they were conferred, then the US government could be justified in removing access to lawyers and the possibility of a trial for those suspected members of the Taliban held in Camp X-ray following the Twin Towers' tragedy on September 11, 2001. It is because many hold these rights to be innate that governments are considered duty-bound to respect them.

4. The consequences of rejecting the idea of a single human nature and holding instead that all nature is created and relative, are profound because without it all human rights

disappear unless they are conferred by a particular society which can then just as easily remove them. Most postmodernists do not recognise this problem. Indeed, they appeal to notions such as 'justice' and 'respect for the other', yet these are precisely grounded in the idea of human rights.

5. Just war thinking is based on the idea of a single human nature – international treaties on the way wars should be fought recognise a fundamental distinction between the combatants and non-combatants. Again this is not always easy to define – for instance, those working in arms factories would be held to be contributing to the war effort but so could taxpayers who supported the war effort financially. Nevertheless, the existence of disagreement about precise definitions does not undermine the fact that there is agreement that a fundamental distinction does exist and that innocent parties in a war must be protected. As human beings they have the right to be protected, unless they are culpable, and do not constitute legitimate targets. Just war thinking does, of course, recognise a distinction between intended damage and 'collateral damage', based on the principle of double effect which says that any action may have more than one consequence. This is what happened, for instance, in the Gulf War when the British and Americans targeted the command centres of the Iraqis even though these had been established in a building where a primary school was situated. Hitting the target was considered to be a morally permissible act, of which the killing of children was a regrettable but unavoidable side-effect. The key point here is that the protection of the innocent is recognised by all governments as an obligation (which does not, of course, mean that they always behave as though they recognise this obligation!). This obligation rests on the assumption that all human beings have 'inalienable rights', chief among which is the right not to be killed unjustly – a right not shared by the animal kingdom. This right signposts a commonly held view that human beings have a 'value' in common by reference to their common humanity.

There will, nevertheless, be those who reject these examples and who will maintain that there is no single human nature, that all morality is relative, that rights are conferred not innate, and that culture is the final determinant of what is right and wrong. There is, it must be admitted, no way of proving that this position is mistaken, but those who hold it must necessarily face its consequences which include the following:

- There is nothing, in itself, wrong with genocide – it is simply the most violent outcome of one culture disagreeing with another and, in itself, there is no moral distinction between kindness, compassion, helping others and genocide. On this view, Mother Teresa and Hitler are morally equivalent as there is no way of judging between them.
- Morally repugnant actions such as female circumcision, child abuse, paedophilia and the like become as acceptable as healing the sick or defending the innocent. Killing the innocent is neither unjust nor is there any consequence to it other than contravening taboos constructed by society. In societies where no such taboos exist, then no offence is caused by the killing of the innocent. Both just depend on the framework of the person or community involved.
- Life has no meaning: any meaning that is claimed is constructed by individuals or communities. Pleasure or self-fulfilment will generally be the highest value and the only valid criteria for morality will be what leads to self-fulfilment – even if this comes from being authentic to oneself or complying with the constructs of the society in which a person lives.
- The role of psychoanalysis is simply to help people live successfully in society. It is a pragmatic goal with no concern for the truth about the human condition or helping people to come to terms with the truth about their lives – it is merely a procedure to enable people to cope with and live in the world.

It may, of course, be that these positions are right, but most people would reject them. Given this rejection, the assumption that it does make sense to talk of a common human nature becomes much stronger. Every human is, of course, different – but every human is also the same. The difference is precisely grounded in the commonality of a single human nature. It is only within this nature that differences of appearance, gender, sexuality, etc. arise. No one would doubt or question that wombats have a wombat nature, no one would doubt that swans have a swan nature (although it may be recognised that different types of swans have somewhat different natures, nevertheless they are still swans), and there seems no good reason to doubt that humans share a common human nature. Once this is accepted, then it becomes necessary to consider what this human nature is. This is a far more complex question.

4

Human Nature

What is it to be human? At one level, the answer to this question is obvious: a human is not a kangaroo, an oak tree or a wombat. A human belongs to the human race: it grows, usually following sexual relations between a male and a female, from a zygote within the female's womb, becomes an adult and reproduces with other members of the human race. Even if this is accepted (and it will become clear that this is far from straightforward), then many questions remain to be answered. In the last chapter, it was argued that a butterfly's egg has the potential to become a caterpillar and then to become a butterfly, but the adult butterfly is not fulfilling its potential simply by existing – for instance, when it is asleep. The same applies to a human being.

When a deer is chased by a lion and is wounded but escapes, it may suffer mauling and its hide may be damaged. It then suffers defects to its hide and perhaps more serious injuries. A rabbit in Australia infected with myxomatosis may become partially blind, consequently suffering the defect of poor eyesight. Physical defects are, therefore, common. They exist wherever an individual member of a genus or species falls short of the full potential of the species in question. The same applies to human beings.

In physical terms humans suffer from many diseases and ailments. Many are born defective – they are not as they 'should be' where what 'should be' is defined in terms of their physical human nature. For instance, a baby born blind, or missing an arm, or with Down's syndrome, or cystic fibrosis is in a way defective. 'Defective' here must not be regarded as a pejorative term – it means that there is a defect present which, if the baby were perfect, would not be present. This certainly does not mean that the baby is not human, nor that he or she will be prevented from developing into an adult human being. What it does mean, however, is that defects are present: the baby is not quite 'as it should be'. This is what so many prospective parents mean when, if asked what sex they would like their baby to be, they reply, 'I don't mind provided it has ten fingers and ten toes'. What they mean by this is, 'All we want is a healthy, normal baby'. It does not mean they would not love their baby if he or she was born blind, was missing an arm, had Down's syndrome or cystic fibrosis – what it does mean is that the parents would prefer their baby not to have to suffer in any of these ways. They would prefer it to be 'normal', i.e. a normal human baby. Normal human babies do *not* have these defects, that is precisely why they are regarded as defects.

Traditional thinking in almost all cultures, and certainly in Christianity, has always recognised this and has seen problems that arise at birth or that occur later on (for instance, blindness, disease or handicap) as defects. People with these defects are still fully human, but they are less than perfectly human in a physical sense. The defects may be much smaller than the examples I have given: I am defective partly because I damaged my eyes using a cheap computer screen more than ten years ago. Others are defective because they have lost all their hair at an early age or because they have lost a breast or their testes from cancer. These defects are no one's fault (although it could be argued that because it was my foolishness in using a cheap computer screen that caused my defective eyesight or in the case of a cancer sufferer because he or she continued to smoke in spite of all the health warnings, then there is a measure of blame attached).

The first way, therefore, in which humans can fall short of what it means to be fully human is by suffering physical defects. Even in the majority of cases where there is no blame attached, these defects will be a cause for regret by all those involved. In the same way, physical defects, of course, occur to all animals and plants.

Humans, like animals and plants, can fall short of what it is to be human in physical terms. However, physical defects do not prevent a person from actualising their potential as a human being because the essence of being human does not rest on purely physical abilities, although the person needs many physical abilities to accomplish the work of becoming.

Human potential as being more than physical

There is, however, another type of defect which relates to humans alone amongst the animal kingdom. It occurs when they use the free will which they alone are held to possess, to choose voluntarily to be less than they are intended to be. When people choose to fall short of their true human nature, defects occur. This needs some explanation.

It has previously been argued that a dormant butterfly is not actualising the potential of a butterfly. Assume that the butterfly had free will – in this case it could be that the butterfly is choosing not to actualise any of its potentialities. It might be a lazy butterfly. As such, it would, voluntarily, be choosing to be less than it was intended to be; it is, therefore, choosing to be defective. The same can apply to human beings, but on a much wider scale. For example, a human that is asleep is not actualising some of the potentialities of being a human (even though sleep is very important and desirable!).

There are a number of ways in which human potential may not be actualised:

1. A person may choose to be 'asleep', even if he or she is awake. In a sense such a person is not fulfilling his or her potential. Imagine a child who has a real gift for music – she is outstanding but cannot be bothered to practise or even play. It is not that she has other interests, it is just that she is lazy and cannot be bothered to do anything. She spends hours each day playing with her Barbie dolls and watching television, but that is all. She might play a few tunes on the piano her parents have provided for her when she passes it, but she does not have the commitment or willingness to invest herself in any dedicated practice. So it continues throughout her life. She grows up as a mediocre individual, a pale shadow of what she

might have been, because she has not bothered to develop her talent. Or imagine a boy who has a brilliant talent for football, but he cannot be bothered to attend practices or even to play. All he is interested in is playing on the latest Play Station™ game – and so it continues throughout his life. In both cases one might say that these individuals are not fulfilling their potential: they are wasting something precious and rare that they have and which others would dearly like to have. Not all talents or potentialities can, of course, be developed but a failure to develop any of one's potentialities is, indeed, a waste.

2. A person may be active and busy, rushing around and achieving a great deal, but that which is being achieved may be of little worth and value. Imagine a photographer who has great talent but who decides to devote her life to being a member of the paparazzi (a photographer of the great and the good) solely because this will make her the most money, even though she has a contempt for what she does and the people whom she photographs. This individual might have developed a talent but chooses instead to misuse or waste it.

3. A person might be solely interested in self – he might make himself the centre of his life with the result that he does not mind lying, cheating, stealing or committing adultery provided it is pleasurable. Such behaviour quickly becomes habit forming and an individual choosing to do this regularly might be considered to be diminishing himself, becoming less than he is capable of being because the wrong talents are being developed.

4. A person may refuse to stop and think what kind of individual she wishes to become. She may fail to realise that she can grow and change by an act of will. This represents a failure to recognise that human beings are not simply the material expression of their DNA conditioned by psychological and sociological factors. They are free individuals who can exercise their will to realise their full human potential if they choose to do so.

5. A person may ignore his moral or spiritual potential (the latter is a controversial term which is far from easy to define) and so

may not come to a full realisation of what it is to be human –
he may effectively remain at the animal level by fulfilling his
physical potential alone but nothing beyond this.

Beneath each of these scenarios lies the assumption that all
humans share a common human nature and that fulfilling this
nature matters. Human nature is measured in terms of
potentialities (with some people having potentialities that others
do not, such as the musical, sporting and photographic talents in
the above examples). If these potentialities are fulfilled, then so
is the human being fulfilled: the individual becomes what he or
she is capable of becoming. If these potentialities are not fulfilled
then there is a real sense in which the individual is diminished.
However, these specific talents, which some may have and
others may not, are grounded in a common human nature which
all share.

This, it is suggested, is the key to a modern approach to ethical
reflection which is able not only to address many of the issues
with which society is today engaged but also has a long history,
going back to Aristotle yet continually affirmed throughout the
Christian and European tradition. As a position that is not ex-
clusively Christian it can be embraced by believers of almost all
religious traditions or by those who reject religion entirely, since
it rests not on revelation to be found in any particular sacred
book or pronouncement but on reflection on what it means to be
human.

Defining what it is to be human

In the past there have been two approaches to defining what it is
to be human. One approach might be to define human beings
according to what they are: a carbon-based life form, a biped
which reproduces sexually, made up of 86 per cent water and a
variety of minerals, descended from a common branch of the ape
family, requiring oxygen to breathe, ingesting a wide variety of
food and excreting waste products either as liquid or in part
solid form, and with a life expectancy of about seventy to eighty
earth years, and so on. This is, at one level, an adequate

definition but most people would accept that it does not come close to defining what is distinctive and important about human beings. Aristotle's understanding of human nature, as previously described, led him to define the nature of any living thing in terms of its potentialities – what it is capable of becoming (the examples of the butterfly and the zygote were used to illustrate this).

The previous section listed ways in which human potentialities may not be fulfilled. This lack of fulfilment has, in the Christian tradition, been expressed in two ways, although the fist of these has, mistakenly, been more strongly emphasised than the second.

(i) Morally wrong acts

The potential of human beings to become what they are capable of becoming is diminished and limited when they commit acts which go against what it is to be human. Thus acts which are held to go against common human nature, such as lying, stealing, adultery, murder, paedophilia, rape, and the like, are considered to be wrong or, to put it in religious language, sinful. Acts are sinful if they go against the nature which, for those who are theistic believers, are assumed to be in some sense given by God. It is, however, possible to leave out any reference to God and simply say that acts which go against human nature are morally wrong.

The Catholic Church has traditionally emphasised sinful acts with dire warnings of what will happen if these acts are undertaken (such as, in the Middle Ages, the threat of thousands of years in purgatory which could be remitted by rich people paying large sums of money to the Church or by other forms of penance). These acts require forgiveness and, since forgiveness is held to be in the sole mediating hands of the Catholic priest, this vastly increased the power of the priests and the institutional Church. Religious believers who adhere to the picture of certain acts as sinful (including many ordinary Muslims, Jews and Christians) believe that God has ordained that certain acts are wrong and anyone who commits them will suffer terrible punishment at his hands. St Thomas Aquinas said that the pains of purgatory are greater than any that can be experienced on earth and declared that hell had to be everlasting so that, for instance, the punishment for adultery could be long enough to fit the crime, and any temporal limit – such as 10,000 years – would result in the punishment being inadequate. Few Christian theologians talk in such terms today and purgatory is regarded, if it is held to exist at all, as a place of cleansing and purification. However, for many devout Muslims, Jews and Christians the picture that they retain is of a God who will punish terribly any who transgress his commands, unless they are forgiven through the mediation of the priests and the institution he has set up to undertake this task. Since no explanation is given of the wider setting in which these condemnations should be understood, it is easy to see why so many people think in these terms. It is, however, a travesty of the thinking behind the Natural Law position.*

The key reason why some acts are considered to be wrong is that they are held to diminish those who perform them, causing them to fail to fulfil their human potential. The acts, therefore, are not wrong simply because of the effect they have on others, but because of the damaging effect they have on the people who commit them. This, however, is only part of the picture and discussion of the wider setting in which ethical actions must be judged is much more clearly represented by the second half of the human nature equation. In our discussion of human nature and its impact on ethics this is the obverse side of the coin, and in view of its importance, it is all the more sad that it is so little emphasised by institutional religion.

(ii) Virtue ethics

Virtue ethics holds that the task of human beings is to become fully what they are intended to be – namely to realise their full potential. Instead of concentrating on the negative side of

---

* The Natural Law tradition of ethics stems from Aristotle and St Thomas Aquinas and is the basis for ethics in Roman Catholic Christianity. It holds that certain actions are wrong because these actions go against what it is to be human, they go against the common human nature which all of us share. This position holds that certain actions are intrinsically evil – they are wrong in and of themselves and cannot be justified by appeal to the consequences of the action or the situation in which it is performed. For more details see *The Puzzle of Ethics* by Peter Vardy and Paul Grosch (London, HarperCollins, 1999).

morally wrong behaviour it emphasises the primary importance of individuals fulfilling their human potentialities to their full extent. The emphasis is on acting to develop virtues so that human potentialities are fulfilled, enabling individuals to become fully human.

Virtue ethics is not so much interested in the question 'What should I do?' but rather 'What sort of person should I become?' It is concerned more with character and the nature of what it is to be human than with the rights and wrongs of specific actions. Virtue Theory seeks to show that there are key virtues that underpin the life of any admirable human being. Since there are many different virtues, all good, moral choices may depend on how individuals rank them and which in their eyes outweigh the others.

Character and disposition are continually being developed through the actions of human beings. Virtue ethics rests on developing a consistency of behaviour in accordance with certain general ethical principles. St Thomas Aquinas held that all actions should be examined, even those that are insignificant. Individuals should ask themselves, 'Are these ways of acting making me more just, prudent, temperate and brave?'[*] Aristotle considered that virtue was a habit, or at least it became a habit if practised regularly. Just as an athlete has to train and practise, so the person who would be virtuous has to train him or herself in virtuous behaviour. It follows from this that whilst normal discussion of ethics concentrates on the 'exciting issues' such as euthanasia or just war or abortion, virtue ethics concentrates more on the day-to-day activities of life and the sort of character which human beings develop. A contrast can be drawn between:
1. the ethics of dilemmas – which uses ethical discussion to decide on how moral problems are to be resolved, and
2. virtue ethics – which seeks to determine the sort of person each individual should become.

The background to modern Virtue Theory lies in the work of

---

[*] Quoted in James Keenan's 'Virtue Ethics' in *Christian Ethics* by B. Hoose (London, Geoffrey Chapman, 2000).

both Elizabeth Anscombe and, particularly, Alastair MacIntyre whose book *After Virtue* has had great influence on ethical thinking in the last twenty years. Anscombe rejected the whole idea of moral duty, particularly the Kantian sort of approach which saw duty as a Categorical Imperative – to be undertaken for itself alone and with no other motivation. She rejects the whole idea that 'duty' should be an end in itself and sees an emphasis on duty as being divorced from the needs and aspirations of human beings. She is recognising that 'morality' like 'charity' can be cold and dehumanising and can become the reverse of what it is intended to be. Alastair MacIntyre has extended Anscombe's approach and provides an excellent analysis of the present ethical malaise in which we find ourselves.

Virtue ethics concentrates on encouraging human beings to act in ways which develop them as human beings so that they move closer to fulfilling their potential. By contrast, talk of morally wrong acts and of 'sin' concentrates on the negative actions which drag human beings down and lead them away from fulfilling their potential. However, neither can be properly understood without the other and they are closely related. Any acts which go against the common human nature diminish individuals. Morally wrongs acts, therefore, should be avoided because they have an adverse effect on those who practise them. If individuals allow themselves continually to commit acts which go against their common human nature they will fall further and further away from fulfilling their true potential. The further they go along this path, the more difficult it is to turn round.

Imagine a two-year-old child who steals some sweets from her elder sister – everyone smiles at the ways of the young child who, after all, is not of an age when she can really understand what she is doing. Then the same child, as a four-year-old, steals a bar of chocolate from a friend. At five she steals a coin from her mother's purse. Nothing is said because her mother wants to show her love and she is still regarded as too young to understand. At seven she steals a hair clip from a shop she visits with her mother and a few weeks later steals a brooch she really likes but which her mother refused to buy her. At eight she steals a magazine and some bubblegum which her mother does not let her have. At thirteen she has graduated to stealing clothes with friends and her group is by now expert at spotting the in-store cameras and distracting the shop assistants. By fourteen she has moved on to music shops and by nineteen she is likely to have no compunction in stealing from her employer. Each of these acts, by itself, is relatively insignificant but, taken together, they form a pattern which gets gradually more and more firmly established and becomes easier and easier to continue.

The Implications for Ethics

Human beings can full short of what it is to be fully human in two ways:
1. physically
2. morally.

Individuals can fail to realise their potential as a person by refusing to develop virtues or by acting in ways that diminish their humanity. What it means to fulfil human potential by free actions is central to any discussion of ethics today. This issue will be discussed in the second part of this book but, in the meantime, the focus will be on the significance for ethics of the acceptance that some physical defects are, indeed, defects and represent the physical side of human nature which is not fulfilled.

5

The Correction of Human Physical Defects

When Australia was first discovered by Europeans, they found many strange animals. The kangaroo, of course, quickly attracted attention but it was some years before the Europeans came to hear about a strange creature which the Aboriginals called by a variety of names – one of which was the 'womb-bat or 'vombat'. It was given the scientific name *vombatus*. This animal was shy and was rarely seen but it could move fast. The first drawings depicted a squat animal rather like a pig and with many young, although it is now known that even twins are very rare. Although knowledge of wombats increased slightly over the years, people did not pay much attention to them. The first serious study was undertaken by a fourteen-year-old schoolboy, Peter Nicholson,[*] in 1960 at Timbertop, the Year Nine campus of Geelong Grammar School, which is set on the side of Mt Buller in an isolated position buried in the Victoria bush.

This young researcher was obsessed with wombats. He would leave his dormitory at night when the other boys and the teachers were asleep and would creep off into the bush to study them. He climbed down their holes, sometimes a long way underground, tying a piece of string to a tree so that he could find his way out again. He got to know individual wombats, and studied how wombat burrows were made. The paper Peter Nicholson wrote for a science fair in Melbourne at the age of fifteen is regarded as

---

[*] Chronicled in *The Secret Life of Wombats* by James Woodfood (Melbourne, Text Publishing, 2001).

one of the best studies of wombats ever produced. Still, today, knowledge of them is limited. It is generally recognised that their breeding pattern involves the male chasing the female in figure of eight shapes for a long distance before mating. They are known to be solitary creatures and can run faster, over 100 metres, than the fastest person on earth. They can manage with less water than any other animal of comparable size and their droppings contain less moisture than those of other animals. Despite advances in knowledge no one would wish to assert that a wombat's nature is yet fully understood. Most people who know anything about wombats would acknowledge this and would accept that the only way we will really come to a deep knowledge of wombats is by studying them in depth (which is very difficult as they live underground, are extremely anti-social and cannot be easily bred in captivity). Some people, of course, will profess to having no interest in wombats whatsoever and will wonder why anyone should bother to devote much of their lives to studying them.

Wombats, then, are complex creatures. However, far more complex than wombats, are human beings – a fact far less readily admitted. Most people would acknowledge that they do not know much about wombats: they do not understand the nature of wombats. Yet when it comes to human beings, it is assumed that they are easy to understand and, what is more, that the generally accepted understanding of them is adequate – but precisely the reverse is the case. We do not even understand the physical nature of a human being (for instance, we have no idea how a human being thinks, or what makes it possible for a human being to do something as commonplace as moving an arm), yet the full complexity of a human being goes far beyond any physical description.

European moral theory is founded on the Aristotelian idea of a single human nature, while the Natural Law tradition of ethics defines human nature according to Aristotle with minor modifications by St Thomas Aquinas. Although this represents a very limited and, in many ways, clearly inaccurate understanding, it is taken by the Catholic Church to be the definitive view of what a human being is. However, if the understanding of what it is to be human is mistaken, so will be the moral precepts which are based upon it.

If there is a common human nature, then certain physical characteristics are common to all human beings, just as certain physical characteristics are common to all wombats. The list is almost endless but it might include:

- two arms, two hands, two wrists, eight fingers, two thumbs, fingerprints on fingers and thumbs – arms, hands, wrists, fingers and thumbs all jointed and connected so that they can manipulate objects or be used for a wide variety of purposes
- one heart, two lungs, two kidneys, one spleen, digestive tract, reproductive organs, all fulfilling their individual function and operating together to enable the human being to engage in a wide range of activities
- two legs, two thighs, two knees, two ankles, two feet, ten toes – all jointed to enable walking, running, skipping, cycling, rollerblading, swimming, etc.
- immune system enabling the body to defend itself against infections
- head, two ears and eyes, one tongue, one nose with two channels connected to the lung; brain with nerve endings extending to every part of the body enabling data to be processed regarding pain, hunger, thirst, co-ordination, sexual desire, fear, and a reflective ability enabling advanced calculations and thought processes to be carried out; hair, eyelids, eyelashes, and so on.

Not everyone, of course, is identical: humans come in a variety of heights, weights, hair and skin colour, build, gender, sexual orientation, and many other factors. Now it could be argued that, because there are these variations, then the whole idea of a single human nature can be dismissed. This, as was argued in chapter three, is too simplistic a conclusion. Wombats vary in much the same way as humans (which is not surprising given that more than 95 per cent of their DNA is identical) but no one would seriously doubt that wombats have a wombat nature, within which there exist minor variations. Similarly, (as previously argued) international law clearly recognises the idea of a single human nature whilst allowing for a measure of diversity. Most factors are common to all human beings and diversity exists within this commonality.

Some human beings, however, are physically damaged. They suffer from defects which are caused in a number of ways. Men and women lose their limbs through war or industrial accidents; some people lose their eyesight as a result of accident, deliberate injury, torture or disease; some women are infertile and their ovaries cannot produce eggs; some men are infertile and cannot produce sperm; some people have two hearts; some people have no immune system so that any infection will kill them; some have brain damage; some have hearing or visual difficulties; some are midgets and cannot grow more than 1.2 metres tall; some have no feet or diseased joints so that they cannot walk; some have no digestive tract as it has been removed due to disease, or they have an abnormality from birth. Then there are the wide range of diseases that attack people. Polio used to be a killer and sufferers could not live outside a heart and lung machine that encased their body. Twenty per cent of the population of some African countries have AIDS; many people have cancer, tuberculosis, cholera, whooping cough, chicken pox, malaria, or the like.

This long list of physical defects is far from exhaustive. These defects represent the extent to which people fall physically short of what a full human being should be. Many, of course, manage very well with their disability whilst others are cured. The very word 'cure' is itself significant. It means that something which was wrong has been put right. The person suffered from a defect which has now been corrected. For others, the condition from which they suffer may, based on present medical knowledge and resources, be incurable – but there is always the hope of advances in medical technology or the (rather vainer) hope of a fairer world where resources are more evenly distributed.

It has taken a long time, but we are now in a position to apply this reasoning to the test case of problems in genetic engineering outlined in chapter two. Once it is acknowledged that:

• human beings share a common human nature, and

- those who are suffering from a physical disability are physically defective compared to the common human nature,

then the language of 'correction of defects' becomes appropriate. No one will quarrel with a surgeon operating to rectify physical defects in a patient's body caused by cancer or by some inherited defect. No one will quarrel with drug treatment to rectify physical damage to a patient caused by a virus. No one will quarrel with using surgery to rectify disorders or defects that arise due to age, such as a hip replacement or even a transplant. All these are now generally accepted.

The transplant case is interesting since, when the first blood transfusions and the first heart transplants took place, many religious groups were suspicious and, indeed, negative regarding these interventions as being 'unnatural' or 'against God's will'. Such first reactions may frequently be attributed to the fact that they stem not from dispassionate analysis but from an emotional reaction.

If the correction of physical defects by surgery, drugs or other procedures is accepted, then there seems to be no essential difference to these same defects being treated using somatic cell genetic engineering.* Unless it can be shown that the risks are notably higher or the risk of damage considerably greater, or unless it can be demonstrated that the interests of others are being negatively affected, then there seems to be no clear ground for opposition. It does not seem to matter whether the engineering takes place at the foetal stage or in later life – in both cases physical defects are being remedied and this is a good thing.

The issue of germ line gene therapy is in some senses very similar but in others notably different. Unlike somatic cell genetic engineering germ line therapy affects the gametes or reproductive cells, namely the ovaries in women and the testes in men. Its benefits may well outweigh those of somatic cell

---

* Somatic cell gene therapy involves the insertion of genes into cells for therapeutic purposes: for example, to induce the treated cells to produce a protein that the body would not otherwise produce and the absence of which may lead to disease. It does not affect the genetic make-up of the patient's children and it also does not change most of the patient's cells.

engineering since it enables rectification not just of the patient's defects but also defects that would be passed on to any future children. It will allow doctors to hold out the hope of not simply ridding individual patients of disorders such as Down's syndrome and cystic fibrosis, but also ensuring that they are not passed on into the gene pool. There seem to be strong reasons in favour of this therapy. If the disorders already described are regarded as diminishing what a human being should be (i.e. they are physically less than is expected from the common human nature), there would seem to be no clear argument to say that it would be better to leave an individual with these physical defects when it is possible to eliminate them.

Indeed, if a doctor could cure a patient of cancer, it would seem to be wrong to refrain from doing so, unless there are other factors to be taken into account. Similarly, it would seem to be morally right, indeed obligatory, to do all we can to rid human beings of inherited defects which lead them to be less than fully human in a physical sense. Significant numbers of young women with perfectly healthy breasts are having both breasts removed at around twenty years of age. They are undertaking this drastic step because they carry a genetic profile which means that the likelihood is that well above 90 per cent of them will develop breast cancer before they reach thirty. There is clearly nothing wrong with preventative surgery which reduces the chance of the early deaths of these women. Equally there seems no reason why there should be anything wrong with eliminating the genetic defect that gave rise to the probability of breast cancer.

Seven arguments could be put forward against this, the last of which is of most significance:

1. It may be claimed that by interfering with the genetic code, scientists are 'playing God', something they have no right to do. However, this does not stand up to examination: doctors interfere all the time. A person who suffers from a heart attack is rushed off to hospital and treated by every means available, including sometimes by a transplant. If the doctors eventually say, 'There is nothing more we can do, it is now in God's hands', what they really mean is, 'We have done everything our present medical science can do. We now have to let things take their natural course.'

By their very decision to create children with another person individuals also have an impact on the genetic code. By deciding to have children with 'A' instead of 'B', 'C' or 'D' an individual is making a decision about the child's genetic make-up. There seems little essential difference between the situation in which a person 'falls in love' with 'A' and decides to have a child, and the situation in which a person decides to have a child with 'A', knowing that the mix of their genes will create deformities in the child and therefore arranging genetic intervention to ensure these deformities do not occur. To say that it is 'natural' to have a deformed child and that it is 'unnatural' to make use of the knowledge that is now available to avoid defects in the child is a weak argument. If these defects can be eliminated at the foetal stage, then there seems no reason to wait until the baby is born to correct them (which, in any case, is likely – once the genetic technology has been perfected – to carry far more risk for the individual). What is more, if one believes in God, then presumably one believes God has given human beings reason and intelligence to be able to cure diseases and other defects. If they now have the tools, using this reason, to be able to rectify genetic defects, there seems no good reason why they should not do so.

2. If someone believes in God then they may hold that every embryo is a direct creation by God. This is the position adopted by the Catholic Church and Pope John Paul II, but there are major difficulties associated with it. The view arose from the traditional idea, originating with Aristotle and historically proclaimed by the Church, that God implants a soul at forty-two or ninety days depending on whether the foetus is a boy or a girl. The man was considered to implant a 'homonucleus' (roughly translated, a 'little man') in the woman's womb or nest but it did not become human until a soul was implanted by God. St Augustine recognised that a fertilised egg did not have the same status as a pre-embryo.* He put it like this:

> If what it brought forth is unformed but at this stage some
> sort of living, shapeless thing, then the law of homicide

---

* A pre-embryo is the name given to the fertilised egg in the period from fertilisation up to fourteen days. Thereafter it is an embryo.

would not apply, for it could not be said that there was a living soul in that body, for it lacks all sense, if it be such that is not yet formed, and therefore not yet endowed with its senses.

This idea was modified in the nineteenth century to hold that souls were implanted at conception. Today no one talks of the implantation of souls but, nevertheless, the idea that every pre-embryo is a direct creation by God is still held. Whatever the mechanics behind this assertion it raises very real problems for those who advocate it since it necessitates an adherence to the view that God deliberately creates babies with Down's syndrome, cystic fibrosis, or the like, and this raises questions about the nature of such a God. The modern proponents of this view – explaining the birth of babies with such conditions, for instance, by saying that it was due to original sin, natural evil or the direct intervention by God – have to face the real difficulty that many defects are now known to be genetic and in many cases directly traceable to the parents. If, then, there is a perfectly good natural explanation for how these defects arise and how they can be eliminated, then bringing God in as an explanation seems irrelevant. 'God' is simply being invoked to explain something that can be explained in scientific terms. It is rather like someone saying 'God did it' when the traffic lights changed from red to green. It seems rather simpler and more plausible to say, 'They changed because they were timed to change in this way'. Similarly, instead of saying that a pre-embryo is a direct creation by God with God having planned the defects, it seems rather simpler, more plausible, and theologically and philosophically more adequate to hold that this is just what happened. This does not rule out belief in God – instead God can be held to have created and to sustain the system through which reproduction takes place.

Some will, of course, find this uncomfortable and will still want to insist that each person is directly created by God. When little was known about reproduction, this position made sense but today it is far more difficult to justify. Few modern philosophers or theologians see a soul as a separate substance, believing rather that a whole human person develops from the moment of fertilisation of the female egg by the male sperm. Once this is accepted, it is still possible to talk of 'direct creation by God' but it will be a way of recognising the uniqueness of each child and as a description of divine activity in creating and sustaining a world in which the miracle of birth is possible, rather than as a way of describing the intervention of God in bringing each individual into existence.

It is also possible to argue that God does not implant souls, but they are rather naturally generated by physical processes. This is a heresy named Traducianism which has been formally condemned by the Christian Church. Christianity has never been a dualist religion and it seems rather easier to maintain that the whole idea of a soul as a separate 'something' is irrelevant to the issue of genetic engineering.

Having said that the idea of persons being a direct creation by God seems to be flawed, it is essential not to draw a mistaken conclusion from this. The rejection of direct creation does *not* mean that every single human being is not unique, special and, if one is a believer in God, of tremendous importance in the eyes of God. This importance is not lessened if direct creation is rejected. God, after all, is held to have created the incredible systems which make DNA and reproduction possible and if the universe is indeed created in order to foster and develop human life, then the preciousness of each life in the eyes of God is not in any way undermined by denying direct creation.

3. It may be argued that by making genetic alterations genetic diversity will be reduced and, since one of the key features of all types of sexual reproduction is sexual diversity, this is not a good thing. This is a cogent challenge but it applies much more to genetic enhancement than it does to the correction of inherited defects which is the area being discussed here. In genetic enhancement genes are manipulated in order to enhance characteristics, for example, in order to produce slim, blonde and blue-eyed babies, It is true that evolution advances by genetic mutations, but there seems no clear genetic advantage in allowing physical defects in human

beings to continue in the gene pool when they could otherwise be eliminated. To encourage defects simply because they are an indication of genetic diversity seems perverse and not easily defendable.

4. Genetic engineering is still in its infancy and mistakes will be made. This is a troubling challenge as it means that mistakes may affect the human being whose genes are being altered and it could make some even more defective than they were before the procedures. Of course, every effort will be made by scientists to avoid this. Exhaustive tests are done on, for instance, mice which are genetically very similar to humans and clinical trials on humans are carefully monitored. Nevertheless, it is true that in the early days of these new techniques there will be unfortunate errors. However, the same has applied to every medical advance and this has never been a reason not to pursue it. There is an understandable wish by many that all medical treatment should be risk free but this is impossible. The possibility of mistakes being made and the resulting baby being more defective than he or she would otherwise be – in spite of the efforts made to avoid this – is particularly hard to contemplate. Naturally the risks and rewards have to be weighed by the ethics committees of hospitals and universities. There will be mistakes and there may be fatalities, but there is no essential difference between genetics and any other area of new medical research and many will hold that the long-term benefits are likely to greatly outweigh the few mistakes that may be made.

5. The 'risk against reward' argument maintains that once germ line therapy is permitted, Pandora's box will have been opened. The altered genes will enter the human gene pool as one cannot stop genetically engineered children eventually having their own children. Whatever the immediate advantages, it may be argued that the long-term dangers are unknown. This is a good argument, but it is only an argument based on our current state of ignorance. It may well be an argument in favour of delaying germ line genetic engineering until we can be more certain that there are no unforeseen

problems: it is not an argument against allowing germ line therapy at all.

6. It may be argued that a child is a gift and not a right and that concentration on the physical basis of reproduction misses out this important insight. The idea of a child as a precious gift to be loved and cherished as a unique individual is vitally important and is at the heart of most religious perspectives on conception. There is a very real danger that babies will come to be seen only in physical terms and to be regarded as commodities to which everyone has a right. There seems no basis for an argument which holds that a woman who goes through the pain and discomfort of IVF to obtain a child does not cherish and love this child just as much as one obtained by so-called 'natural' means. Both women can equally cherish their children and regard them as a gift and, even if genetic alterations are carried out, there seems no reason why the love a man and a woman have for their children should be undermined.

7. Germ line genetic alteration will require experimentation on embryos or stem cells derived from embryos and, since every embryo is a person, it can never be right to experiment on one person for some possible benefit to others. This is a difficult area and needs more detailed examination.

There are two crucial issues underlying point (7).

(i) Is an embryo a person?
This is a vexed question and is not easy to answer. It raises major philosophical issues, which it is beyond the scope of this book to debate. The key issues are as follows:

1. Is a dualist or a monist view of human personhood to be adopted? A dualist maintains that a person is made up of soul and body and these two interact. A soul is implanted into living matter at birth and at death the soul separates and goes elsewhere. Plato and Descartes are the best-known examples of dualists – both maintaining that the real 'me' is my soul. As we have seen, Catholic tradition taught, following Aristotle, that souls were implanted by God at forty-two days in the

case of male foetuses and ninety days in the case of female –
prior to this the entity present in the womb was not a person
but merely a *homonucleus*. In the 1975 Declaration on Abortion,
the Roman Catholic Sacred Congregation for the Doctrine of
the Faith stated that, although it could not be established with
certainty that at conception the entity is already a human
person, nevertheless this may be the case. Abortion, then,
would be committing murder. Although the Church no longer
talks of implantation of souls, Pope John Paul II clearly stated
that every human person is a direct creation by God and must
be treated as a person from conception. The difficulties
associated with this position have been dealt with above.

2. A monist maintains that a person cannot be split into soul and
body but is an indissoluble unity. This is the more commonly
held view. It gave rise to the findings of the Warnock Report on
which British legislation is based. The report points out that
fertilised eggs can split (to form identical twins) up to fourteen
days after fertilisation takes places and it is also possible for the
split egg to come together again. If, therefore, a person is
regarded as an indissoluble unity, the possibility that the
fertilised egg could split into two, forming two people, or that
the divided egg could also come together again to form one
person, means that a fertilised egg cannot be regarded as a
person. For this reason Warnock concluded that personhood
status could not be awarded until fourteen days after conception, forming the basis for British legislation which allows
research on embryos up until the fourteen-day mark.

If the issue is considered in terms of potential, it seems clear
that the fertilised egg does have the potential, subject to certain
conditions being met, to develop into a person. It may not be a
person (just as a caterpillar is not a butterfly nor an acorn an oak
tree) but it does have the potential to develop into a full human
being. If, therefore, what it is to be human is defined in terms of
potential, it would seem that fertilisation, despite its ambiguity,
is indeed the best point at which to confer personhood status. A
fertilised egg could then be regarded as a potential person but
not necessarily be treated as an actual person as there is a

morally significant difference between a fertilised egg and a full human person. This is clearly brought out in the Aristotelian analysis already outlined. Just as an acorn is a potential oak tree but it is not an oak tree, so a fertilised egg could have the potential to be a person without being a fully actualised person. As the potential becomes increasingly actualised with development, so the developing entity becomes more worthy to be treated as a person. Most people would want to say that there is a morally significant difference between an adult human being and a fertilised egg because the adult has actualised more of the potential to be human than a fertilised egg and needs, therefore, to be treated differently. This is recognised in nature where sixty per cent of a woman's fertilised eggs do not implant but are wasted within ten days of their period. These fertilised eggs are potential people but the potentiality is not actualised. The fact that the Christian Church does not baptise embryos miscarried in the early stages of pregnancy, is an implicit recognition of a morally significant difference between the developing pre-embryo and the fully developed child.

Even if, however, *both*

(a) full personhood status is conferred at conception *and*

(b) it is considered necessary to treat the embryo as a full person rather than simply a potential person (which seems, at the least, a highly debatable position),

this does not necessarily rule out embryo research because much depends on the ethical system that is applied.

(ii) Deontology versus proportionalism or consequentialism

A distinction needs to be drawn between two broad ethical theories:

1. The first is deontology. Deontologists maintain that certain acts are always wrong whatever the circumstances. If it is accepted that all human beings have a common human nature, then any act that goes against this nature is *intrinsically evil* and no appeal to consequences or circumstances can justify it. People who take this line, for instance more conservative Catholics, maintain that certain actions are always wrong irrespective of the circumstances in which they are

performed. For instance, it might always be wrong to use the morning-after pill as, in the second half of a woman's cycle, it would be considered to be an abortion. Thus, Pope John Paul II condemned the use of the morning-after pill even in the case of gang rape of young teenage women such as occurred during the war in Kosovo. In this view the situation and the consequences are irrelevant – if an act is wrong, then it is wrong, and must not be carried out.

2. The second theory embraces two views which are similar but different: the proportionalist and consequentialist views.

(a) Proportionalists hold that the particular circumstances in which an act is performed must be taken into account in judging its moral status. If, therefore, the Nazis are at the door asking if there are any Jews in the house and Anne Frank is upstairs, then in this situation lying might be the right thing to do. Similarly, cutting open a woman's stomach may be a good act if it is part of life-saving surgery but an evil act if it is intended to cause her death. The rightness or wrongness of an act cannot be judged without taking account of the context in which it was performed.

(b) Consequentialists say that what makes an act right or wrong is the consequences or effects it has. Thus it might be right to lie to save the life of a Jew who is hiding from the Nazis, or to help an old, terminally ill person who is in constant pain and who wants to die, to do so. Both involve taking the context into account and the effects of the actions in deciding whether they are right.

In the case of both these views, the fact that an embryo *is* regarded as a human person, would not rule out experimentation. The Jesuit theologian Karl Rahner put it like this: 'It would be conceivable that, given a serious positive doubt about the human quality of the experimental material, the reasons in favour of experimenting might carry more weight, considered rationally, than the uncertain rights of a human being whose very existence is in doubt.'[*]

---

[*] *Theological Investigations* (London, Darton, Longman and Todd, 1967).

Thus, although certain actions may be wrong (and the doubt that Rahner expresses about the state of the embryo rightly draws attention to the lack of certainty), in some cases the benefits they produce, are likely to be of such magnitude that they outweigh their possible wrongness. This can be argued to be true of genetic research. Some, of course, will disagree, maintaining that certain actions are wrong in themselves and nothing can make them right. However, life is not that simple, and circumstances are vital in determining whether an action should be performed. Even if, therefore, a pre-embryo is regarded as a full person rather than a potential person, the benefits of research may well outweigh the damage caused.

Another factor that may count in favour of experimentation on pre-embryos up to fourteen days arises from IVF techniques. IVF has made it possible for many women who in the past would never have been able to have children, to do so. The success of the procedure in individual cases is still far from assured, the procedures are unpleasant, and the failure rate is still high, but nevertheless tens of thousands of children have now been born as a result of it. The procedure involves extracting about twenty or more eggs from a woman, fertilising them and then re-implanting two or three in the womb in the hope that at least one will implant. This raises a key ethical issue. Since only two or three of the fertilised eggs are implanted, the remainder are destroyed. If it is considered that a fertilised egg is a person, this would be considered as murder, one of the reasons why the Catholic Church condemns IVF. Another reason is the fact that the man has to masturbate to produce the semen to fertilise the egg and masturbation has traditionally been held to be an intrinsically evil act. Most non-Catholics and many Western Catholics, taking the proportionalist or consequentialist view, consider IVF to be morally acceptable in many cases. If these arguments are accepted and IVF is allowed – as it is in almost every Western country – then spare fertilised eggs will be generated and most couples will generally be only too happy for them to be used for research purposes. Once this principle is accepted, stem cells from pre-embryos will become relatively widely available and will be able to be used for research. This would challenge the argument that the use of pre-embryos for genetic research is morally wrong because embryos are readily available as a by-product of present IVF techniques.

The Implications for Ethics

These various arguments can now be put together. If it is accepted that human beings share a common human nature, then correcting physical defects by either somatic cell or germ line gene therapy would seem to be not just morally acceptable but morally good acts. The key proviso would be the 'risk against reward' argument, i.e. it must be possible to show that the potential risks do not outweigh any immediate advantage. This argument may cause the delay of the genetic engineering of human embryos because the unquantifiable risks have not yet been fully assessed, but this would only be a delay until a fuller assessment was complete.

The most effective criticism might have been that this would involve experimentation on pre-embryos but at most it would seem that these are potential people rather than full persons. Even if it was insisted that they were full persons, then a consequentialist or proportionalist approach to morality could still justify experimentation of such pre-embryos because of the likely benefits that will result in eliminating human defects.

However, it is one thing to allow genetic engineering in order to correct physical defects, it is quite another issue to allow it in order to enhance physical characteristics. It is to this thorny issue that we will now turn our attention.

6

The Physical Enhancement of Humanity

Somatic cell and germ line gene therapy seem likely, in the future, to be able to be used both to remedy defects and also to enhance various physical characteristics. Some of the most obvious examples of this come in the sporting field. The Australian swimmer Ian Thorpe is referred to as the 'Thorpedo' – he is the fastest swimmer on earth and continually breaks new world records. However, Thorpe has size seventeen feet, and it has to be recognised that this is equivalent to swimming with flippers. Anyone entering a swimming competition with flippers would be laughed at and banned, but no one can raise any questions about natural ones! It will soon be possible to breed future swimmers with big feet. The procedure used to achieve this, enhancement genetic engineering, is very different to the correction of defects discussed in the previous chapter. To put it in more popular terms, we have now moved into the realm of 'designer babies' – babies that have been specifically designed to meet the wishes of their parents.

There are many ways in which parents may wish to enhance the characteristics of their offspring. Some parents may want:
- a particular eye, hair or skin colour
- to develop intelligence
- to develop particular musical abilities
- to develop athletic abilities.

It is not yet known how much, for instance, intelligence, or musical or sporting ability is genetic but there is every reason to believe that there may well be a strong genetic link. If the link is established, then in principle it should be possible in the future to enhance any of these characteristics. It will not be easy – these characteristics are unlikely to stem from any single gene and charting the complex genetic paths that influence behaviour will take many years. What is more, these abilities may come at a price that will not be easy to determine, since change in one area may have negative effects in another. However, the fact that it is likely to be difficult does not mean that it will be impossible. For instance, we already know that sporting ability seems to run in families and the child of two sporting parents may well also have sporting ability.

This whole topic raises, of course, the time-old debate in education between 'nature' and 'nurture' – how much of human intelligence, sporting and musical abilities are due to individual natures (in other words, to what extent are they genetic) and how much do they depend on nurture, the way people are brought up, or the influences on them as embryos in their mother's womb and beyond.

It also raises the issue of dispositions to act in certain ways. Some have suggested that there are genetic links to violence or aggression, or even dispositions to alcoholism or to criminality. The debate is wide open. All that can be said at present is that it looks as though both nature and nurture play a part.

How, then, does the principle of a common human nature illuminate the arena of enhancement genetic engineering?

In the last chapter it was argued that the rectification of physical defects at the genetic level would seem to be morally acceptable. Does the same apply to enhancement? Is it ethical to breed 'super children', with physical characteristics that exceed the normal? These are not easy questions. Already such individuals exist – they occur naturally. There are people with great physical ability, high intelligence, attractive appearance, and many other positive features. And clearly they are human beings in exactly the same way as those who are physically defective are. If it is considered morally right to rectify defects so that the maimed, deformed or defective child is made normal, is it also acceptable for the average child to be made 'better' in a physical sense?

Take two individuals, Luke and Sam:

- Luke is tall, attractive and intelligent with an IQ of 125; he is physically excellent, has a strong resistance to disease, and also has considerable sporting and musical ability.
- Sam is of average height, has a tendency to put on weight, is average at sport, is tone deaf and has an IQ of 100.

If we now introduce another individual, Benny, who is similar to Sam except that he has Down's syndrome, then what would our attitude be to the genetic alteration of these three individuals? In the last chapter it was argued that genetic alteration at the embryo stage to rid Benny of Down's syndrome would be a morally good act. Down's syndrome represents a physical defect and eliminating this defect would be a good act. However, would it be morally acceptable to enhance Sam so that he was more like Luke? Luke clearly has advantages over Sam, just as Sam has advantages over Benny. Sam's advantages over Benny can be expressed in terms of defects which Benny has but which Sam does not. Can Sam be described as being defective in comparison with Luke?

These are questions that it is not easy to answer, and that raise the idea of a master race of 'gen-rich' people whose genetic profile has been enhanced. Expressed in these terms, the immediate reaction of many people is likely to be negative to any idea of enhancement genetic engineering. However, the Lukes of this world do exist naturally, as do the Sams. Unless it is argued that only what happens naturally is right (a position that it is very difficult to maintain as it would mean that it is not morally right to rectify defects which occur naturally from birth), then why should Luke have characteristics that Sam does not have?

Many Western governments recognise that some children can be termed 'talented and gifted'. They have potentialities that others do not and, therefore, are often provided with special education to foster their talents. These talents are 'natural'; they are the result of the genetic interchange between their parents and cannot presently be predicted. But the time may soon come when parents are able to choose to have children who are talented and gifted as a result of genetic selection.

Imagine another two individuals, Sarah and Sally. Both are tall and intelligent; both are well co-ordinated and good at sport; both have musical ability. However, Sarah lives in Europe and Sally in sub-Saharan Africa:

- Sarah is one of two children. She is well fed and well clothed, goes to playgroup and plays with stimulating toys. Sarah is inoculated against a range of diseases and her diet is balanced and well planned. Her parents are wealthy so she attends an excellent school with superb facilities including training in two musical instruments. She has access to a computer at home and by the age of seven is regularly using the Internet. She gets her first laptop at twelve and has a mobile phone. Sarah travels widely and grows up in a safe, comfortable en-vironment. She is aware of the world and even as a teenager has some appreciation of the global picture and of her place in it. After leaving school she will go to university and then go on to train as a doctor or a lawyer. Her life expectancy is eighty years.

- Sally is born into poverty. She is one of ten children, three of whom died within a year of birth. She has had no inoculations and had several serious diseases when young, one of which left her face pock marked. She will go to school until the age of ten but then she will have to work on her parents' small plot of land. She walks for four miles each day to get water for her mother and often does not have enough to eat. She cannot read or write, will be married at thirteen, and will have her first child at fourteen. Her life expectancy is forty-five years.

Money has bought Sarah advantages that Sally could not dream about. Genetically they may be very similar, but their lives will be hugely different because wealth has brought advantages to the one which the lack of wealth has denied to the other. This inequality is generally accepted and few challenge the power that money brings. Even within the Western world, Sarah will have advantages that poor children in the same country will not enjoy. If, then, it is morally acceptable for money to buy educational, musical, sporting, technological, travel and health advantages, then the question can be asked: why should it not also buy genetic advantages?

Some may wish to argue that, although economic inequality results in such disparity, this is not the way it should be. The present status quo is imperfect. Money should not buy advantages in life and there should be equal funds available for educating children in the third world as there are for children in the first world. However, this is a utopian dream, as parents will always seek to provide advantages for their children.

Once money is allowed to buy certain categories of advantage, it is difficult to argue that other types of advantage should be ruled out. The claim that parents should not have the chance to buy private education for their children, private health care for themselves or other privileges, is impossible to maintain. All parents naturally want the best for their children and will use their own position to improve their children's lot. Even in a supposedly egalitarian society, those at the top of the power heap will ensure that their children have advantages that others do not enjoy. The theory of equality is a splendid one, but it simply does not work in practice. The only truly equal communities may be monastic ones or communes, but even there hierarchies are formed with, for instance, the abbot or abbess having privileges that ordinary members of the community do not have.

Once the general principle of privilege is accepted, then there seems no good argument for preventing people buying genetic privilege for their children. In fact, this privilege has always existed as those at the top of the economic pile are often the most successful genetically, and they will form relationships and have children with others at the top of the pile – thus ensuring their children have a reasonable chance of a natural advantage. Alpha males tend to have children with alpha females and this means that there is a high probability (not, of course, a certainty) that their children will be genetically privileged. Once it is accepted that wealth can in general buy privilege, then genetic privilege is merely one more example.

Certain religious groups will argue against genetic engineering on the grounds that, since every child is a direct creation by God, no tampering should be allowed. However, in the previous chapter it was shown that this argument really does not work.

First of all, the mechanics on which the argument is based are either flawed or, at the least, far from clear. No serious theologian maintains any longer that God implants a soul into every fertilised egg and, as we have seen, the idea of souls being naturally generated has been condemned as a heresy. Our knowledge of genetics makes it possible for us to explain conception as a natural process, rendering it very difficult to find a direct role for God within it – unless it is argued that, at the moment when every sperm enters every egg, God interferes and manipulates the interchange of chromosomes. The majority of theologians would reject this thinking which relegates God almost to the 'god of the gaps' and seeks to locate God's activity in an area which science has yet to explain. God is no longer thought to 'tinker' in human processes in such terms. There is, however, a more devastating argument against the idea that every person is a direct creation by God.

There is now overwhelming evidence in favour of children being genetically related to their parents. Simple tests are available to determine paternity. The people of Iceland have taken part in a unique genetic study through which, because of their excellent birth and marriage records, the transmission of genetic disorders can be traced back over hundreds of years. If, then, God is held to have a direct role in creating each individual human being, God would have to be constrained by the genetic make-up of the individual's parents. This would radically diminish the significance of God's role. At the most, it would be confined to a fairly minor 'tweaking' – small alterations to factors that are largely determined by genetic inheritance, or to ensuring that a certain sperm out of the two million possibles (the approximate number produced in each ejaculation) wins the six-inch race to fertilise the egg. And if God is held to 'tweak' genes, on what basis would this intervention be carried out? On what basis are some children genetically inferior and some genetically superior (within the limited room for manoeuvre left by the genetic input of the parents)? And why would God choose to make some embryos genetically defective? It could hardly be based on the virtue or vice of the embryo. The alternative to laying genetic defects at God's door is to lay them at the parents' door as a result of sin – a return to a form of theology which has thankfully long since been abandoned by most thinking individuals.

It seems altogether more plausible to say that, if there is a God, God creates and sustains the evolutionary system through which life evolves but does not intervene continuously in the process. This is, of course, a position that some religious people will find difficult to accept: for instance, it runs counter to the teaching of the Catholic Church which has always maintained, and still maintains, that every human being is a direct creation by God. However, as the previous chapter made clear, this view in no way diminishes the value of every human person.

One argument which casts doubt on the future of enhancement genetic engineering draws attention to present ignorance on the effects these procedures may have. Owing to our as yet very imperfect knowledge of the genome, we simply do not know what effects alterations in single genes or strings of genes will have on the wider personality of a human being. Any alteration which looks 'innocent' in that it may have no broader effects (for instance, change in height, hair colour or even intelligence) may in fact have profound and unforeseen consequences. This argument will not always hold true, but will be valid whilst our knowledge remains as rudimentary as it is at present. The possible risks of such genetic alteration for cosmetic reasons do not seem justified whilst it is still unknown how far-reaching the effects of enhancement genetic engineering may be. Where rectifying defects is concerned, I have argued that the long-term benefits may outweigh possible risks in the procedures but the same cannot be said of those undertaken for largely cosmetic purposes. Rather, in this case, the burden of proof that there are no long-term effects may reasonably be expected to be even higher and it would seem right to maintain that no approval should be given for such procedures until there is an exceptionally high level of confidence that there are no unforeseen problems. In practice, this may be a difficult requirement to meet, which may mean that it is right to delay approval for enhancement genetic engineering for a considerable time.

A more general but associated argument is related to bonding between parents and children. According to this argument, the more tenuous the genetic links between parents and children, the more the natural ties and affinities may be reduced. The natural bond between mother and child and, although perhaps to a lesser extent, between a father and child, is based partly on the genetic links and partly on the natural processes and shared responsibilities involved in the child's upbringing. (The fact that adopted children often have very strong links to their adoptive parents indicates that it is important not to exaggerate the contribution of genetics.) As the mother carries the baby in her womb* and breastfeeds, and as mother and father care for the child, changing nappies, feeding, playing, interacting, educating and the like, the bond grows. It can be argued that if genetic links are weakened so that children eventually can be designed to order, they may come to be seen not so much as a gift and a privilege but a designer commodity rather akin to a smart car, expensive computer or a new house. This may devalue the idea of the child as a full human being, deserving of love and respect in his or her own right simply by virtue of being a human being. Instead the child may come to be valued (or not valued) on the basis of his or her characteristics. This is well brought out in the film *Gattaca* which portrays two brothers, one who has been born naturally and one who is gen-rich. In the film genetic tests at the age of thirteen determine the future fate of adults – some become high flyers (in the film they become astronauts), others carry out the more menial practical tasks (in the film they become cleaners).

In contrast to these apparently weak arguments against enhancement, those in favour appear strong. Foremost among them is an argument provided by the theory of natural selection which is the means used in the natural world to ensure evolutionary success. The 'survival of the fittest', which was first documented by Darwin, is now well established as by far the

---

* Although within the next twenty years it seems likely that women's wombs may become unnecessary as it may become possible for a foetus to be grown from conception to 'birth' in an incubator. This development would considerably weaken the bond between mother and child.

most plausible theory to explain how all animals and plants have evolved. Apart from a small number of religious conservatives (particularly in the United States) who reject natural selection and evolution and consider every species to be created directly by God, almost all serious and internationally recognised thinkers (including theologians and philosophers) accept the truth of evolution. If natural selection fosters diversity and increasing complexity in the natural world, then it is entirely possible for those who believe in God to hold that evolution is the means used to achieve this purpose. There is, of course, much room for speculation as to why a God would use a means which is built on one species tearing another apart and the success of which depends on the consignment of countless different species to oblivion. However, such speculation does not undermine the widely recognised fact of evolution.

Just as the evolutionary success of human beings – evolving from common ancestors which they share with apes – was marked by their initial ability to use tools and to employ their intelligence increasingly to dominate their environment, there seems no reason why human beings cannot now use their understanding of the human genome to develop their species still further. It would seem entirely logical for human beings to continue to use their reason to help their species evolve.

Even if one believes in God, this conclusion – which to some may seem radical – makes great sense. If there is a God, then God has given human beings rational minds to enable them to make moral decisions and to develop medical technology and other resources to help them to live in harmony within this world. Indeed, it is held to be one of the crowning glories of human beings that they do have these faculties. Once this is accepted, then to set limits to how this intelligence should be employed seems arbitrary. There has been a tendency in the past for religious people to be nervous of new developments. However, if they believe God has given human beings minds, then it seems perfectly proper to argue that these minds can be used in eliminating disease and physical defects and also in enhancing human beings further to enable them to fulfil their full capacity, by employing the genome in appropriate ways.

As part of the ongoing debate there will be a need for ethical reflection on what it is to be fully human which will facilitate decisions on the limits to any proposed enhancement.* Excesses can easily occur and the problems of deciding what may and may not be acceptable will not go away – but this is not the same as ruling out enhancement engineering in principle.

It would, for example, be morally wrong to choose deliberately to produce people who are defective. There have already been cases where deaf couples have wanted deaf children, and it would be easy to imagine blind people wanting blind children, and so on. There is a strong desire for parents to make children in their own image. So far, this has been achieved through IVF using parents with the correct genetic make-up, for instance, using those who are deaf to seek to ensure that deaf children are produced. In principle it should eventually be possible to achieve the same result using genetic engineering. Under the argument of this book, it would be morally wrong deliberately to create individuals who are less than they are capable of being. To choose deliberately to create physically defective individuals – whether the defect is deafness, blindness or deformity – is a denial both of the common humanity of all human beings and of the aim of helping each individual to fulfil his or her full human potential both physically and, as will be discussed in the second part of this book, spiritually.

This raises, of course, the difficult issue of whether it would be morally right for a homosexual or lesbian couple to choose, if this should become possible using genetic engineering in the future (and this is a highly debatable assumption), to create a homosexual or lesbian child.† If there is a single human nature, then there would seem to be a good case for saying that this human nature is heterosexual. Once this is accepted, then the

---

* This may well be a task for the ethics committees of some hospitals but it will certainly be one that needs to be undertaken by moral philosophers and theologians working with the latest insights available from a range of disciplines including psychology, psychiatry, physiology, biology, medicine, anthropology, theology and philosophy

† It is far from established that sexual orientation is linked to genetic make-

deliberate creation of homosexual- or lesbian-inclined individuals would be a morally wrong act as such inclinations would seem to run counter to the normal expectation of a common human nature. This is not in any way to condemn those who have such sexual preferences but it is to accept the wisdom, grounded in the Natural Law tradition, that such inclinations are a 'privation of good' – they do not represent the best of what human nature is intended to be. This also does not make any judgement about whether those who have such inclinations are morally right or wrong to engage in sexual practices which are in accordance with this nature. This is a separate issue which is not dealt with in this book.‡

It is important not to misunderstand what is being said here. If there is a single human nature, then helping individuals to be rid of defects is morally good and similarly a case can be made for enhancing individuals so that they reach their full human potential based on a single, common human nature. This argument cannot be used to justify the creation of defective babies simply to meet their parents' particular desires – the yardstick of working towards developing children who are, physically, in accordance with a common human nature or common human potential is central and creating defective children to suit their parent's whim is morally wrong.

The Implications for Ethics

There would not seem to be any convincing argument against either germ line or somatic cell genetic engineering to remove physical defects *or* to enhance specific human characteristics. The arguments in favour of the removal of defects through

---

up. Various studies have been attempted to establish this but none is conclusive. It may be that sexual orientation is linked to testosterone imbalance in the early months of pregnancy but here too the evidence is ambiguous. What does seem clear, however, is that such orientation is not simply a matter of choice by the individual concerned and that physical factors are, at least partly, involved.

‡ This issue is dealt with in *The Puzzle of Sex* by Peter Vardy (London, HarperCollins, 1997).

genetic engineering seem to be strong. There may be a case for delaying enhancement genetic engineering for much longer than some may consider desirable because of the unknown effects such enhancement may have.

The real danger, however, of the whole discussion about the use of genetics to remedy defects or to enhance humanity is that it takes the discussion away from the really important issues that need to be addressed. There is much more to being human than purely physical features and this is where the real significance of the argument in this book lies. It is one thing to discuss the issues of genetic engineering in relation to what it is to be human but this cannot and must not be done apart from the far more significant and far more profound issues which will next be addressed. The real danger of such discussions is that genetic engineering will be isolated from broader considerations of what it is to be human and this cannot and must not happen.

PART TWO

*Whilst genetics are important, discussion of genetics
and physical characteristics alone cannot come close
to an understanding of what it is to be human.
Indeed, the real danger is that it will obscure
this understanding.*

7

What Is It To Be Human?
Who Am I?

Two ways of answering one question

One way to answer the question 'What is it to be human?' is to reply entirely in physical terms. As we have seen, some people fall short physically, and this gives rise to the whole array of ethical issues arising from genetic engineering, some of which have been dealt with in the first part of this book. However, few people would consider that any physical description can come near to providing a complete answer to the question 'What is it to be human?' or the related question 'Who am I?' The answer demands much deeper reflection and, indeed, no clear answer seems possible. Human beings know an increasing amount about the universe and this planet, they are beginning to understand something of their genetic code and the environment in which they live, but they seem no closer to understanding who they are as human beings than they were two thousand years ago.

To begin to answer the question 'What is it to be human?' or even the more specific question 'Who am I?' will not be easy. Yet, if human beings share a common human nature, and if this common human nature is to provide a basis for ethics, then an attempt at an answer must be made. In addition, if the task, as Aristotle and the European tradition have always considered, is for each individual to 'become fully human', then it is imperative to have a clear idea of what this means. In order to try to come to a closer understanding of what an answer might look like, it may be easier to concentrate initially on seeing if any answer is possible to the second question, 'Who am I?'. This is the task of the second part of this book.

The very question 'Who am I?' raises questions – because in many ways the answer is obvious. One possible definition is solely in terms of roles. A person may be a wife/husband, mother/father, teacher, business person, committee member, sister/brother, child, doctor, supervisor, student, or fulfil a myriad other functions. In some roles a person may be reasonably successful, in others a complete failure, and in most probably somewhere in between. Most people would define human beings in terms of their roles. However, talk of such roles does not get anywhere near to answering the question 'Who am I?' It does not begin to answer who we are independent of these roles: who is this self that I am?

I remember having dinner one evening in the City of Norwich with a close friend whom I had known for many years. At the end of the dinner this friend asked me: 'What do you mean by "becoming a self?", we are all selves. We all have jobs and friends and relationships. What more do you think there is?' I could not answer the question adequately, and I remember being angry with myself at my inability to do so. I was convinced that there was much to be said on this subject and that being a 'self' went far beyond a description of roles. However, explaining what this 'more' was to someone who did not accept there was anything more to describe was something I was not able to do with any clarity.

In the play *Waiting for Godot* by Samuel Beckett a young boy is asked if he is happy, and he replies, 'I don't know'. Even after surprised questioning his reply remains the same. He has no idea how to answer the question. The two heroes spend the duration of the play waiting patiently for Godot to arrive – only he never comes. They fill the vacuum of time talking and come to recognise that all their thinking seems futile. They even begin to doubt whether thinking itself is of any benefit. They 'blathered about nothing in particular' and recognised they had been doing this for half a century. They cannot move from where they are because they are waiting for Godot. 'What are we doing here?'

they ask each other, but they have no answer. They are stuck in a static limbo. Their condition is very similar to that of all human beings.

Plato provided one of the most famous stories in philosophy when he asked his hearers to imagine that they were in a cave, tied to chairs facing a wall. Behind them a great fire burned, and between them and the fire people were going backwards and forwards and their shadows were reflected on the wall. The captives took these shadows for true reality and, because they did not know anything else, they were content. According to Plato, the task of the philosopher is to release him or herself from the chair and to find the way out of the cave. This will not be easy and, in fact, the very attempt will be difficult. If they succeed and make their way out of the cave, they will be blinded by the sight of the sun (which for Plato represented the Form of the Good) and they will come to see the world of the cave as a mere shadow. The title of the play about C. S. Lewis, *Shadowlands*, is based on Plato's cave. Plato considered that if those who had escaped out of the cave attempted to return to release prisoners, the prisoners would be angry with them and would refuse to listen. They would not want to hear that the world they inhabited was not the real world.

A very similar image is given in the classic science fiction film *The Matrix* in which everyone is living in a world just like ours going about their busy lives. A very small number of people, outsiders to society, come to recognise that this is not the real world, but a monstrous illusion. Everyone has been deceived, and the first and most painful and dreadful task is to awaken to this reality.

Plato's story of the cave or the imagery of *The Matrix* can be dismissed by rejecting the assumptions on which they are based. Plato assumed a world of absolute ideas, Forms, in contrast to which this world was merely a pale imitation. Postmodernism and developments in philosophy over the last two thousand years have raised doubts about this picture and few today would support Plato's theory of Forms. Similarly, few would accept the idea on which *The Matrix* is based of human beings living in a computer-simulated world produced by intelligent machines.

However, even if these assumptions are rejected, the human condition may nevertheless still be very similar to that portrayed by Plato and *The Matrix*. The need for individuals to awaken from their slumbers may still be great.

Postmodernism, indeed, affirms this. It claims that we are in the grip of coercive forces that seek to impose values that destroy local cultures and attempt to impose a global hegemony. Individuals are asleep and need to be awoken to this reality. Postmodernism is often seen as subversive of traditional values and old certainties, but this should not be seen as a criticism so much as a positive claim. It tries to show the truth of the human condition, a condition that is complex, multi-faceted and free from certainties. Indeed, one of the greatest lessons that postmodernism has taught is that certainty is an enemy rather than a friend; certainty provides a security that is an illusion and is false.* It is precisely in ambiguity and a recognition of complexity that truth may lie and nowhere is this clearer than in the moral sphere.

Socrates wished to be a gadfly, in order to wake people out of slumber. He tried to challenge the habit and routine which had deadened the lives of the citizens of Athens into a comfortable mediocrity. They were the living dead whom Socrates wished to awaken. The middle-class citizens of Athens rejected Socrates and his questioning, but many young people related to what he said. Two thousand three hundred years have passed since the time of Socrates and it would be easy to assume that human beings have advanced since then, but this is debatable. We have grown in understanding through philosophy and science only to come back to Heraclitus and the realisation that everything is in flux, everything changes. There appears to be no meaning, no truth – the quest for these, like the quest for the holy grail, seems to have been in vain.

The greatest challenge that Socrates faced was that people did not wish to be woken up. They were comfortable in the lives they were living and did not see the need to change – still less to

---

* See *What is Truth* by Peter Vardy (Alresford, John Hunt Publishing, 2003).

ask themselves uncomfortable questions. It is not surprising that the middle-class citizens were the greatest critics of Socrates since they had the most to lose. Accepting that their comfortable lives were empty would have forced them to reappraise their whole way of living.

Socrates' response was to teach by questioning, by attempting to get people to see for themselves, but he also recognised that there was no guarantee that they would do so. He was using what Søren Kierkegaard, the Danish philosopher, theologian and psychologist,* called indirect communication. This involves trying to get people to see something, not by lecturing at them but by opening windows which may allow them to come to an understanding that they did not have before and which cannot be conveyed in any other way.

Returning to the definition of human beings according to their roles, it could be, of course, that once one has listed the things a person does, the roles he or she plays, and the things he or she owns, then there is nothing more to be said. However, most of us would deny that this was the case and would want to affirm that 'Who am I?' is the most important question in the world. Jesus asked what it would profit a person if he gained the world and lost his soul. To talk of soul here is to talk of a person's identity, and Jesus clearly recognised that it was possible to lose this identity – to become nothing at all, to become a cipher, a copy of every other human being, a vacant shell.

Most people would accept that the 'Who am I?' question is important, yet in almost every school classroom, at most universities and in most people's lives, this question is neglected. It is a question about which most people seem to show no interest at all. For some years I have worked with schools across Australia in an attempt to improve religious and values education in the country. We built into the curriculum of some of the major schools time for silence and stillness. As part of this time, young people were asked to consider the question 'Who am I?'

---

* Wittgenstein described Kierkegaard as 'the greatest thinker of the nineteenth century - and a saint'. Part of the argument in the second part of this book owes much to Kierkegaard's insights.

and then to reply to this either in confidential diaries that only their teacher saw or else by using art or other techniques. It rapidly became clear that to many young people the question itself did not make sense. They defined who they were in terms of what they owned and what they did – not in terms of any deeper identity that did not depend on roles.

Many education systems are now 'outcome driven'. Teachers have to state aims and objectives for every lesson and for every course, and on completion have to measure whether these aims and objectives have been met. The aim of education, then, becomes something that is measurable in terms of objective outcomes and this culminates in examinations or assignments which test whether the input by the teacher has been absorbed by the pupil. The more traditional, and now seemingly old-fashioned and broader, view of education went much beyond this. Having said this, there never was a golden age – but there have always been good teachers. One problem in education today is that teachers' hands are tied so that they cannot teach as effectively as they would like. They cannot easily engage the humanity of the children in their schools.

People will ask someone who is about to leave school or university, 'What are you going to do?' but they will never ask, 'What sort of person are you going to become?' Even if they did, hardly anyone would know how the question might be answered. The emphasis is all on success that can be measured – usually in financial terms. Thus the highest paid professions tend to be the most highly desired and highly respected. Medicine and Law degrees are some of the most in demand as both provide a sure route to financial success. It used to be the case that other occupations were respected due to the contribution they made to society – teachers, civil servants and priests were prime examples. Their social standing was high even if their income was not and joining these professions was seen as a vocation. Today the very word 'vocation' or 'calling' is almost a thing of the past. If society wants more teachers, then the only answer given is to pay teachers more. Increasing salary is intended to increase the desirability of the profession and thus to increase the number of applicants. At one level this all makes complete sense, yet it also misses something of great importance.

Unless individuals are prepared to engage with the 'Who am I?' question at a psychological and spiritual level rather than simply at a material level, something of crucial importance in the understanding of what it is to be human is missed. No amount of description of roles or genetic make-up can answer the psychological questions about the nature of human existence. These psychological questions merge into spiritual questions and neither can be cashed wholly in material terms.

If we define ourselves in external terms, in terms of what we do, what we own or even the relationships we have, then who we are becomes radically contingent. Our very identity can be destroyed if these roles and possessions are taken away from us. In fact, of course, this is exactly what happens in unemployment, retirement or sometimes divorce. Some examples will illustrate this:

A highly accomplished and able nurse worked for many years in the poorest of third world countries where she had exceptionally high levels of responsibility for large groups of people as well as for very substantial medical aid budgets. Eventually she decided to return to her home country but she found, when she came back, that all her experience counted for nothing. She was now out of date – medicine in her Western home had moved on and she had none of the certificates that were required for a job in the Health Service. The only way she could get a job was by going back to the very bottom, effectively emptying bed-pans, in an overstretched system which she found uncaring and in-efficient. She tried, but she could not bring herself to 'play the game' that the system required and found herself out of work with no money. She wandered the streets in the day time and told her few friends what it was like not to have a job - her identity had disappeared. People looked through her. She had no role and she was invisible.

A Catholic priest stepped down from his priesthood on con-science grounds. He could no longer accept the recently increased power of the Catholic Magisterium and did not believe in what he was now being called on to teach. He had been a priest for twenty years – respected and looked up to. He was chairman of many committees, lived in a substantial presbytery and had someone to cook and clean for him. Once he stepped down he had nothing, literally nothing. He had no money, no income and no skills. At the age of forty-eight, he was out of work and had nowhere to go. He eventually found a job selling double glazing on the telephone and had just enough money to rent a bedsit in a poor area. His old friends dropped him and he found that his identity was destroyed.

Many women now postpone marriage and children because they are building successful careers. In their mid twenties they feel that there is 'plenty of time' and whilst they may have a number of relationships, they are aware of the danger of relationships going wrong so they postpone commitment in the hope of finding 'Mister Right' in the future. However, women more than men have the problem of a fast-running biological clock and the situation at thirty is very different from that at thirty-six. At thirty-six time can seem to be running out and many women are faced with an invidious choice – either to marry someone whom they may like but who is less than ideal, who may be a good father but is somewhat predictable and boring, or to hang on in the hope that a real soul-partner may emerge. The trouble is, of course, that the ideal man may never come along and by the time a woman is thirty-six she may well be looking at men who have had a number of failed relationships or who have had difficulties forming relationships. This can impose very real pressure with all options seeming unattractive. In addition, a woman in this position may be seeking her fulfilment and, indeed, her essential identity through someone else and if this someone does not emerge, then a hidden despair can easily result.

Many women who care for children wake up at the age of around thirty-five to forty to find that they have lost any sense of individual identity. They have become subsumed by their roles. They are wife, mother, driver, cook, cleaner and probably have at least one paid job such as teacher, doctor, shop assistant or lawyer – but who *she* is as a person seems to have disappeared from the equation. When once her partner talked about the meaning of life and cared for her as an individual, now the talk becomes simply a matter of practicalities and, if she allows herself to think about herself at all (and it is all too easy for this to seem selfishness and a luxury), then she may come to despair of her existence. She ostensibly 'has everything' in the outward sense but has 'lost everything' in the inner sense of having lost her very self, her soul.

Retirement is frequently a time of crisis when the identity that people have built up through their jobs and through the accompanying contacts are taken away. Suddenly people in this position have to live with themselves and, with time on their hands, they cannot avoid facing themselves. What they often see is an empty shell. Their lives are devoid of meaning and they gaze into the future with dull despair. On many occasions, of course, they will find new sources of activity – for instance, taking an active role as grandparent, working for a charity shop or taking up a hobby such as golf. In taking on these new activities they create a new framework of meaning for themselves.

The above examples do not, of course, mean that all those facing unemployment, retirement or lack of relationships are in crisis. What they do indicate, however, is that if these individuals are honest with themselves (something that it is difficult to be) they may well find, if they allow themselves the time to raise the question, that their lives appear unsatisfactory. The reason may well be that if one finds one's identity in externals, then, when externals go wrong (as they almost always do), one's very identity is threatened.

Defining who people are in external terms fits very well with defining what it is to be a human being in terms of genetics since both genetics and external roles and possessions are easily measurable and quantifiable. In fact, however, this limited approach with no reference to the psychological or spiritual dimension of what it is to be human masks a lack of identity, a lack of self-hood. People who do answer like this or for whom externals are their only marks of identity may not be selves at all – instead they are what they do and what they own or are determined and defined by those with whom they are in relationships. Take these away and they face a vacuum. This 'vacuum', this lack of meaning, will lead to despair – a despair which is often not recognised or which goes unnoticed. Despair is often portrayed in negative terms and yet it will be argued that it can be highly positive as it may point individuals to the fact that the life they live is empty. It is worth being clear that 'despair' here is not being used to mean depression or feeling unhappy – it is being used in a much deeper sense than this. It represents a malaise at the heart of existence where hope is a distant dream and necessity seems to rule. These themes will be explained and developed further in a later chapter.

What is a self?

Many people wear masks. We are chameleons, adapting ourselves to the new people or places in which we find ourselves. The person we are at the office, at university or at school may be very different from the person we are with our husband or wife, lover, father or mother-in-law. The oldest excuse in the book for a man contemplating adultery is to claim, 'my wife does not understand me' but, in fact, few people are understood by anyone else. Instead, they show themselves to others with their reality filtered by the masks that they consider will make them acceptable.

The skills and techniques for doing this are developed very early on in school or playgroup where the desire to be accepted and to conform is very strong. Any mark of idiosyncratic behaviour is likely to be met with disapproval. This is evident in the television programmes schoolchildren watch and the clothes they wear. The desire not to be thought 'different' is deeply ingrained and quickly learned. Difference is likely to bring disapproval and rejection from the group. Of course, some who are very firmly grounded in a group (for instance, by showing excellence in a team sport, at music or, less often, in the classroom) may find the strength there to be a leader or a trendsetter in other areas but even being a trendsetter requires that others will follow the trend set. Someone who is not particularly good at anything and who tries to be different will quickly be isolated. People learn early in life to retreat behind their defences and to wear masks, not to let anyone else see them as they really are. A young thirteen-year-old boy put this very well in a poem:

THE WALL
They laughed at me.
They laughed at me and called me names,
They wouldn't let me join their games,
I couldn't understand.
I spent most playtimes on my own,
Everywhere I was alone,
I couldn't understand.

Teachers told me I was rude
Bumptious, overbearing, shrewd,
Some of the things they said were crude,
I couldn't understand.
And so I built myself a wall,
Strong and solid, ten feet tall,
With bricks you couldn't see at all.

And then came Sir,
A jovial, beaming, kindly man,
Saw through my wall, and took my hand,
And the bricks came tumbling down,
For he could understand.

And now I laugh with them,
Not in any unkind way,
For they have yet to face their day,
And the lessons I have learned.
For eagles soar above all birds,
And scavengers need to hunt in herds,
But the lion walks alone,
And now I understand.*

---

* By Adam Butlin, in *The Hospice Book of Poetry* (St Helena Hospice, 1992). It is a sad reflection on today's world that a number of those who read this poem immediately wonder whether the teacher might be a paedophile. Suspicion is becoming so ingrained today that the idea that teachers can simply be doing their job out of a sense of vocation, dedication and a wish to help young people realise their potential becomes treated with scepticism.

This young boy learnt a painful lesson and retreated behind a wall to protect himself. However, he was lucky enough to find a teacher who understood and who helped him come out from behind his wall. Many others build their walls and, behind these walls, their real selves die until all that is left is the mask they have created. Since this mask is generally formed from achievements in the objective world, the result is that any real sense of selfhood has disappeared.

Many people have no sense of having lost their selves, indeed they have no conception of what it is to have a self. This is an issue which they have never thought about and which has never arisen for them. They are active and busy, they make money and buy a house and car, and the question 'Is this all there is?' is never really allowed to arise for them.

Abraham Maslow, in 1954, suggested seven needs that human beings have which, if they are satisfied, will ensure that their lives are fulfilled. At the most basic level these are physical needs but at the higher levels the needs become psychological and are much more difficult to satisfy being closely tied in the individual's realisation of their full potential as a human being. The stages are as follows:

1. *physiological needs* – the basic drives of hunger, thirst, shelter, sleep and sex
2. *the need for safety* – safety from physical danger and physical anxieties
3. *the need for love and belonging* – the need to belong to communities or groups and to be able to give and receive love
4. *the need for esteem* – the need to be respected and accepted by others and also the need for self-respect which comes through achievement and competence in whatever field to which the individual has dedicated him or herself
5. *the need for knowledge* – the search for meaning, the desire for understanding and knowledge of the world and the human condition
6. *aesthetic needs* – a yearning for beauty in art and nature as well as for symmetry and order.

Finally comes:

7. *the need to self-actualise* – this represents a human at their full potential, someone who has become fully human.

Maslow was a humanist and did not have any place for God or the transcendent in his thinking but, nevertheless, the analysis is helpful. Most people become stuck at the lower stages and seek to satisfy themselves with belongings or reputation. These inevitably disappoint, and yet people do not know the causes or sources of their disappointment.

People who locate their identity in the roles and tasks they undertake remain in the lower levels of Maslow's stages. They have no internal psychological or spiritual identity and all that is then left is the created external identity. This results in a lack of consistency that could be provided by a clear, internal focus and a centre which could remain unchanged no matter what the outer circumstances. The lack of such a focus means that it is the outward, objective circumstances that determine who a person is. Such individuals may indeed be highly successful in their career, be a good family man or woman, have many hobbies and yet, in a real sense, they may have lost their 'self'.

What is most terrible of all is that people may not even be aware that they have lost their self. Any other loss they would certainly notice – if they lost their wife, their house or their career they would certainly notice. But the loss of themselves passes away as if nothing had been lost at all.* The more successful a person is in life, the more likely it is that this loss may take place.

If human beings have no centre to their life, nothing for which they would be prepared to make a sacrifice, nothing for which they would live or die, then they have lost any sense of identity except that provided by their activities and their possessions. There is a real sense in which they are failing to fulfil their

---

* Søren Kierkegaard, writing under the pseudonym 'Anti-Climacus', in *The Sickness unto Death* (London, Penguin, 1989) put this as follows: 'in the world, a self is what one least asks after, and the thing it is most dangerous of all to show signs of having. The biggest danger, that of losing oneself, can pass off in the world as quietly as if it were nothing; every other loss, an arm, a leg, five dollars, a wife, etc. is bound to be noticed' (pp. 62–63).

human potential. They have grown to be adults physically but that is all. Their true human potential remains unrealised.

A person without a centre may not be able to love in any real sense. Of course, anyone who was accused of this would angrily deny it and all of us probably firmly believe that we can love (just as we would believe we are a self), but if our lives have no centre, there is no real self at all, nothing that can love in any deep way. People without a centre may, of course, continue to do the things one would expect as outward signs of love – such as remembering birthdays, springing unexpected surprises, making love, bringing up a family, sending flowers at special moments and caring for their partner, but love goes beyond this. Indeed, this is a good illustration of the difference between the outward and the inward. If all that love consists of is 'doing things', then there is no internal side to love. To really love someone means caring for his or her soul, for his or her deepest self, and one can only do this if one has a self or understands what a search for this self is about. Otherwise all one has is 'loving behaviour' which could be performed equally as well by a well-programmed robot as by a human being.

The Implications for Ethics

Once human beings are defined in terms of their genetics and their roles in life, then the whole psychological and spiritual side of what it is to be human is ignored or neglected. What is worse, there is no inner core or centre from within which ethical judgements can be made. Instead:
- the world happens to the individual,
- the world presents itself,
- the world then determines the individual and his or her values.

In the absence of any inner spiritual or psychological core, there is no place from which to make independent judgements. Since identity is dependent on the way the world presents itself, the world determines who individuals are and how they will react to it.

In the absence of any psychological or spiritual centre, ethical reflection becomes merely a matter of identifying with any passing external framework or transient internal or external impulses as there is no inner centre from within which judgements can be made. Faced with a multitude of ethical dilemmas, it is hard to find any reference point to resolve them. What is more, even individual opinion is not something that an individual has arrived at for him or herself. It is, rather, the result of the cumulative views presented by the media and group influences. The danger of this is that those who inform the group become all powerful leading to the media being the real determinant of ethics.

The power of the media and the group is shown clearly in the way democracy is manipulated by the media and financial interests. Democracy sounds an admirable idea since in theory it represents government by the will of the majority, but it has real dangers. Politicians appeal to what are often the lowest common interests of the majority and standing for what is right becomes difficult in the face of what is expedient and popular. Apathy can easily be produced as individuals feel that their vote is of no consequence and, therefore, they feel no responsibility for whomever is elected. Democracy was condemned by Plato and has many more disadvantages than most people admit or recognise. It can easily provide a cover behind which individual responsibility can be dissolved and, instead of each individual having to be responsible for his or her conduct, the group now takes centre stage as the government is elected by 'everyone'. The power of the media to influence the majority has never been greater. This is seen most clearly in the United States and in many third world countries where money controls access to the media and the candidates who control the media are most likely to do well. The media and the elected government can influence and to an extent determine what is and what is not morally acceptable. People come to believe that if they are doing what others do, then they are acting ethically.

If individuals do not have a psychological or spiritual core, then power and media groups easily sway and influence them. The power of the community or the group with which they identify then becomes decisive. This is because, without a psychological sense of being a self, there is no place from which the individual can make ethical judgements. Indeed, the self itself does not exist as a self – it is a mere copy or a construct erected in conformity with the changing whims of the individual or of the community with which it identifies. Those in a position of power in communities or groups are consequently able to generate mass support and enthusiasm for the most unlikely policies – this applied in the case of Nazi Germany, in the communist regimes in the former Soviet Union and its satellite states, in Pol Pot's regime in Cambodia where nearly two million teachers and middle-class people were killed, in Rwanda where Hutu families willingly took part in the murder, rape and pillage of their Tutsi neighbours following long government propaganda, in the Taliban in Afghanistan, and even in fundamentalist religious groups. However, it is not simply in extreme situations where the power of the group is dominant and where the power moulds and forms those who belong to the group. In today's capitalist societies the media dominates and acts like Big Brother in George Orwell's *Nineteen Eighty-four* to ensure conformity with the proclaimed world view.

In capitalist societies the ability of the media and culture to convince people that meaning will be found in 'lifestyle choices' or in acquiring things is quite extraordinary. So successful are these campaigns that they are not even questioned. Television programmes watched by millions are devoted to renovating houses with new designs or re-planning gardens. These 'lifestyle' programmes are a mere symptom of the widespread view that the things that are owned have direct and central relevance to who a person is. On this view, people are expected to find meaning in acquisitions or dreaming of acquisitions. However, these are never satisfied because the objects desired are incapable of bringing satisfaction. The Buddha recognised this most clearly when he taught his followers that the root of all suffering lies in desire, and that this desire needs to be eliminated.

When individuals do not have a strong sense of self, then community or shared values become the means of finding identity through acceptance. Communities will identify with particular sections of the media which will reinforce the group opinion as to what is important and what is and is not acceptable. In almost every country it is possible to name particular newspapers, radio shows and television channels and then to have a fairly good idea of the sort of people who will watch or read them. Even within religious groupings (such as Anglican, Catholic, Muslim, Buddhist, etc.) different publications will support different perspectives and people will buy the publications that reinforce their world view rather than those which challenge and question this perspective.

The tendency will be for people to watch and listen to media that confirm their existing opinions or which 'form' these opinions in ways that are considered 'acceptable'. What is acceptable, of course, is in itself determined or strongly influenced by previous media and society views. In spite of this, opinion can and may be changed by argument or debate, but all too often people are unwilling to engage with arguments that run significantly counter to their own. The power of the media to dominate or at the least to influence opinion is a central modern element in undermining individual autonomy and contributing to lives which have no centre. This can result in people who are adults physically but who fail to fulfil their human potential because they are not selves.

Not everyone, however, fits into this category of people whose lives are dominated by externals and who have no inner centre. There are those who do have a clear psychological centre to their lives, who are 'selves', who have reflected on existence and who have the capacity to live their lives out of a clear inner orientation which does not vary with circumstance but is at the centre of everything that they do. Such centres can be broadly categorised under three different headings and in the next two chapters two of the three different psychological centres that can exist will be explored.

8

Living for Self

If human beings are more than their physical make-up, then what type of person they are, what type of self they create, is central to understanding what it is to be human.

What really drives human lives? Clearly, there is no single answer: human beings are complex creatures. As was argued in the previous chapter, many people have no centre to their lives at all. They seek to conform and wear a multitude of masks to make themselves acceptable in the many different situations in which they find themselves. However, not all human beings are like this. Many have reflected carefully on their life, on what they want and what they desire. They are thoughtful, and have a clear psychological centre to their lives. They do not drift as their lives have a firm fulcrum around which their whole being and life revolves – this fulcrum is frequently themselves.

People who have thought deeply about life may simply decide that they are the only people who really matter and that, therefore, social conventions are simply irrelevant unless they serve to increase personal happiness. Why, after all, should they sacrifice their own happiness or their own wishes for some abstract ideal which is merely a construct of society? If individuals have come to the view that there is no God, that there is no meaning, and that there is no morality except the morality society constructs, then they may well decide that to live for self is the only rational way to proceed. This view has a long history going back to some supporters of the philosophy of Epicurus, and today it finds expression in varieties of ethical egoism where all ethical decisions are held to be fundamentally self-centred.

Those who live for self alone have existed in all societies and at all times but, perhaps, they may be more numerous today than ever in the past. There are various reasons for this. Firstly, the old certainties have disappeared, communities have broken down, and in a postmodern world all that seems to remain is meaning that is constructed – stories human beings tell themselves. Secondly, in the modern world far fewer people live in communities than ever before. Divorce is common, and one bedroom and studio flats lead to an increasing sense of isolation. The extended family has nearly disappeared and old people are increasingly consigned to nursing homes. Each individual becomes an autonomous unit, and even their relationships are temporary and are recognised as such.

Nietzsche gave one of the clearest philosophical expressions to the view of life which sees each individual as the centre of his or her own life. As set out in chapter one, by declaring that 'God is dead' Nietzsche was not simply rejecting the God of traditional Christianity, Islam and Judaism in the way that an atheist might. Instead, he was rejecting a way of looking at the world: the possibility of a God's eye view, an absolute perspective from which the world can be viewed. With the death of God goes the death of all absolute values. God dies, and so does metaphysics, Truth, Goodness, Justice and Virtue. Any idea of absolute Truth is, according to Nietzsche, as dead and as futile as God. This led on to postmodernism and the understanding that there are no ultimate truths to be sought – everything depends on the perspective of the person who is doing the viewing.

For Nietzsche morality itself is a sign of decadence* because it holds onto the view that there are such things as values, virtues and good and evil. In his view, no such things exist except in so far as we have created them. 'God is dead' because human beings now recognise God as something which we have created. With this recognition, all those things which the word 'God' stood for, such as absolute value and truth, die as well.

Nietzsche did not consider that life had any aim or purpose. However, he believed that exceptional human beings have to

---

* *Ecce Homo* (London, Penguin, 1992), p. 272.

reach the point where they endow life with a purpose or aim. The aim of all human existence is the production of the Superman, the man with a will to power. The Superman moves beyond the categories of good and evil, which are no longer held to have meaning; he lives life to the full in the face of meaninglessness – he lives life for self.

Not every life lived for self will be quite as blatant as the one Nietzsche advocates. The life devoted to self alone may take many forms and it may well not be outwardly visible. The person who lives for self may not reveal this at all – on the outside he or she may be moral, respectable, appreciate the arts, and go to church, yet, underneath all these possible activities lies the ego. Being respectable, conforming to a moral code, appreciating the finer things in life, such as good food, art, music, the theatre, may all simply be means to personal pleasure. The moral code may be followed but only so long as it is convenient, and it will be broken as soon as self-interest considers this to be expedient. What is desired is not necessarily obvious. The key factor is what is the real centre of a person's life, not what appears to be the centre. Often this real centre is the ego.

Individuals may seem committed to their job, devoted to their family, and be a good friend to those they know but, underneath the outward appearance, what they are really committed to may be themselves. It may be through their job that they obtain pleasure and ego-satisfaction, through their family that they receive affirmation and security, and through interaction with their friends that they feel affirmed and valued. Of course, there is nothing wrong with feeling affirmed, finding satisfaction and enjoying what one is doing, but the key question is the underlying motivation. Many people will do everything in their power to avoid asking themselves questions about what really motivates them as the answer may be too uncomfortable. No one wants to find that, like Narcissus, the centre of their lives is themselves – it is not a particularly attractive picture to present to others, let alone to discover about oneself! This does not, however, prevent the picture being true.

Love is a good test. It is not clear what love means, but perhaps a distinction can be drawn between people or things whom or which a person loves and the person or idea with which a person is 'in love'. The meaning of words are flexible and there may be no agreed definition, but it can be argued that an individual cannot be in love with more than one person or value at a time. A man may well love a number of women or a woman a number of men. We may describe ourselves as loving our job, our family, our friends and our hobbies. But if we claim we are 'in love' we are making a claim of a different order. It means the person, the activity or the ideal is the total centre of our being. This is why it would seem bizarre for people to claim to be 'in love' with their job or hobby or to claim to be 'in love' with two or three different partners. Instead, it would make rather more sense to claim to be 'in love' with one partner. If beneath the surface of busy lives, what a person is really in love with is him or herself, then he or she can be rightly said to fall under the heading of placing self at the centre.

Of course, almost all of us would deny the charge that we are in love with ourselves. It would mean that every other activity, person, relationship or function in our lives has an instrumental value – in other words they are only means to some wider end, namely self-satisfaction. It can, of course, be argued that ultimately every action is selfish and that even unselfish actions are done from hidden but nevertheless fundamentally selfish motives. It is for this reason that counselling and psychotherapy can be so helpful – provided, and only provided, that their object is to uncover the truth about oneself. Sadly, today, much psychotherapy does not have this as its object, but seeks instead to construct a story about the individual in therapy that will enable the person to live with him or herself. This is termed constructivism and is the psychological equivalent of some versions of postmodernism, founded on the view that all reality is constructed and truth is also a construct. Psychologists who take this view do not seek for a true understanding of the human condition but merely seek to enable their clients to cope with the world in which they find themselves. Their approach is essentially pragmatic and denies that there is any truth to be sought, but seeks instead to provide the individual with a constructed story by which they can live and through which they can make sense of their lives. The challenge that the ego so much dreads is thereby avoided and what is fostered is what the ego desires.

The ego, like a hungry animal, seeks to be constantly fed, to be affirmed, to be told it is in good order and is praiseworthy and worthwhile. Anything that fosters a sense of wellbeing will be welcomed by those of us whose centre is ourselves because we are likely to have constructed a vision of reality which places us at the centre and we see ourselves as being fundamentally praiseworthy and to be valued. Indeed, what those of us in this stage will find most threatening is any suggestion that we are not worthwhile, that our lives do not have value, or that we are self-centred. Such suggestions will be suppressed or rejected. What is more, such a negative picture may also be rejected by any friends and colleagues we may consult – all they will observe is our outer masks and few will be able to see through them to the real person. That is why any who seek truth should be indebted to those who are critical of them as their insight may provide an opportunity to re-evaluate motives. The ego is brilliant at producing an image that will foster its own development and will conceal from itself and from others the real nature of its activity and the fundamental selfishness of all its actions.

Few people have followed the God Apollo's injunction to 'know thyself'. This was the inscription over the temple of the God Apollo in ancient Greece and the importance of knowing oneself is as great today as it was 2400 years ago. Yet the journey to self-knowledge is long, painful and hard and is one that few people are willing to undertake, particularly as their egos tell them that it is not necessary. In all our busyness and activity we fail to find the time to be quiet and to be willing to look at ourselves at all, convincing ourselves that the lives we live are worthwhile and that self-examination is a waste of time. All the great religious traditions have been aware of this tendency in the human person to self-deception.

The writer of the book of Ecclesiastes makes this clear:

> Vanity of vanities, all is vanity and a chasing after wind ...
> vanity of vanities! All things are vanity! What profit has man
> from all the labour which he toils at under the sun? One

generation passes and another comes, but the world forever stays . . .

I said to myself, 'Come, now, let me try you with pleasure and the enjoyment of good things.' But behold, this too was vanity. Of laughter I said: 'Mad!' and of mirth: 'What good does this do?' I thought of beguiling my senses with wine, though my mind was concerned with wisdom, and of taking up folly, until I should understand what is best for men to do under the heavens during the limited days of their life. I undertook great works; I built myself houses and planted vineyards; I made gardens and parks, and set out in them fruit trees of all sorts. And I constructed for myself reservoirs to water a flourishing woodland. I acquired male and female slaves, and slaves were born in my house. I also had growing herds of cattle and flocks of sheep, more than all who had been before me in Jerusalem. I amassed for myself silver and gold, and the wealth of kings and provinces. I got for myself male and female singers and all human luxuries. I became great, and I stored up more than all others before me in Jerusalem; my wisdom, too, stayed with me. Nothing that my eyes desired did I deny them, nor did I deprive myself of any joy, but my heart rejoiced in the fruit of all my toil. This was my share for all my toil. But when I turned to all the works that my hands had wrought, and to the toil at which I had taken such pains, behold! all was vanity and a chasing after wind, with nothing gained under the sun. (Eccles. 1:2-4; 2:1-11, New American Bible)

Having indulged himself and tried everything possible to please himself, the writer of the book of Ecclesiastes has found that everything is futile, everything is pointless. All is vanity and no matter how he seeks to make meaning for himself in the world, everything turns to dust.

The Buddha constantly emphasised the importance of stillness and meditation as the route to self-mastery. He said that it is only when individuals are still that they can see themselves as they are and can begin to overcome the bundle of selfish desires that determine their lives. Desire, the pursuit of ego, is, for the

Buddha, the fundamental malaise affecting all human beings and, until the reality of this is recognised, an individual cannot begin to change. Individuals are in bondage to their desires which control them and keep them in a state of illusion. Until this can be accepted and until there is a wish to overcome this state of affairs, bondage will continue. The Buddha emphasised that the path to the wisdom that can begin this journey is a long and hard one that few will wish to undertake.

The aim of meditation is to enable individuals to learn to control the mind, rather than letting the flitting mind control them. Human beings are not simply their minds: their minds can be controlled and directed. The aim is to find peace and stillness, and through this wisdom or enlightenment. The Eighth Stage of the Noble Eightfold Path is Right Concentration or Meditation, which leads to tranquillity. Mainstream Buddhism outlines four stages on the path to tranquillity:

1. The first stage generally is achieved through a monastic or at least meditative life where insight and reflection can be developed. This state can bring an initial stage of joy which is much deeper than mere pleasure.
2. The second stage brings a development of the joy together with peace, calmness and serenity of mind.
3. The third stage involves the disappearance of passion. Individuality ceases to matter and, indeed, the person in this stage may no longer want to live not because they wish for death but because desire has ceased.
4. The last stage brings complete peace having transcended all worries and even earthly joy (this is *Samadhi*).

Through meditation the individual frees him or herself from distractions and from the limitations imposed by the ego. As such, it has no ethical value in itself: it is a means to an end. Through meditation, emotions such as anger, greed and hatred can be controlled in order to first recognise and then overcome them. The ultimate aim of meditation is the achievement of nirvana, when all desire has been eliminated. This is not, as Western critics of Buddhism sometimes maintain, the same as extinction, rather what is extinguished is the bundle of desires that lie at the heart of the ego, by which individuals allow themselves to be dominated.

Crucial to Buddhism is the need to recognise the distinction between appearance and reality – not least in terms of the self. Individuals have to find the wisdom to recognise that the way they appear to themselves is not what they are. Unless they can recognise this ('right knowledge') and desire to change it ('right intention') no progress as a human being is possible. Many people never get to the stage of realising the extent to which they are in bondage to their ego.

Once individuals do begin to recognise that the way they appear is not what they really are, that their lives are centred on ego and all their noble pictures of themselves are false, then the real trouble begins. Such insights into the human condition open up vast chasms of meaninglessness and despair which fundamentally threaten the self-image individuals have constructed and can in some cases lead to emotional and psychological crisis. Life is seen to be empty and to have no meaning. All the aims and activities with which a person has filled their lives dissolve, leaving a vast sea of nothingness. What is in fact happening in this case is that individuals come to realise that they have no real self at all – they had attempted to construct a self on the terms set by their own ego but in reality they cannot sustain this construct in the face of the reality of the world.

Jesus made the same point when he asked what it would profit a person to lose his or her own soul. To talk of the soul here is to talk of the self. Although those who live for self do have a psychological centre to their life formed by their ego, because this centre is the ego, when analysed, it will dissolve and be seen to be empty, or will be seen for what it is. To create a self centred on one's own ego is to live a life constructed on a vacuum, an empty, constructed story.

Pride is a central feature of those in this state of existence. Pride stems from the reality that is constructed by individuals in an attempt to give meaning to their lives. When this construct, on which their life is centred, begins to break down, their automatic reaction will be to try to reinforce it all the more. It is their pride which makes people refuse to accept that the construct they have attempted to establish cannot endure and must be abandoned. This is well illustrated in the story of Mozart's opera *Don Giovanni* when the Don, having lived a self-centred life, comes face to face with death and is about to be led off to hell. He is given the opportunity to repent and to recognise that the self-centred life he has chosen is false and a grave mistake, and that the inevitable consequences of the choices he has made in his life is hell – permanent exile from love. The consequences are inevitable because he has made himself into the sort of person who would be content nowhere else but hell. The only alternative is to face the mistake he has made and to accept that his whole past was built on sand – he has lived a life based an error. This requires recognition of the mistake or, to put it theologically, it requires repentance. However, Don Giovanni's pride is at stake and he cannot – or will not – recognise it. He cannot bear to recognise that the self he has constructed is false. The price is simply too high so he goes to hell by his own decision because his pride will not allow him to repent.

Pride is an exceptionally strong emotion. One of its chief functions is to keep the ego at centre stage, to ensure that concern for self is the individual's chief motivation and that nothing is allowed to threaten the ego. When any such threat is faced, pride rejects it by reinforcing that the ego's picture of reality is the correct one, convincing the person that alternative views must be dismissed. It goes further than that, however, as pride causes individuals to see other people and other situations from their own point of view and to reject alternative interpretations which may threaten the central place accorded to their own perspective.

There are various ways in which this state of existence can be brought about. A state of impenetrable pride and self-assertion can, for example, arise under the following circumstances:

1. If the whole of a person's life is centred on ego, then the ego becomes so strong, so powerful, that it will not allow itself to be undermined, challenged or rejected. The ego becomes so much in control that no alternative view will be accepted, no alternative possibility considered. The ego has become as hard as rock, unable to accept love except on its own terms of self-

control, unable to be vulnerable to another except by maintaining power over the other, unable to love another except in terms of using the one supposedly loved for his or her own ends, incapable of being unselfish except where appearing to do so is in fact an act of selfishness.

2. Some people seek to be open, to be vulnerable and to love, but then they are hurt, they are betrayed. They trusted others but their openness and vulnerability is abused. Their reaction may then be to close down, to refuse ever again to be vulnerable and to set up impenetrable barriers or walls that nothing can break through. Such a person may decide that to be open, to be vulnerable, to trust others is too big a price to pay as the emotional hurt and damage from being rejected is simply too great. Growing as a human being involves risking the self and this the person who is centred on self refuses to do. They consider that the only person they can really trust is themselves and so they retreat behind a fortress mentality. If this position is maintained, the person may die as a self, as the self can no longer develop or grow. The defensive barriers are now so high that nothing can penetrate them. The self-image that the ego has created to preserve itself becomes irredeemable, incapable of being changed. The person becomes harder and harder, less able to show feelings or emotions, incapable of growth or change (even though this may not be apparent to others) and eventually the person becomes so locked in that they have effectively died as an individual. C. S. Lewis put this well in his discussion of love:

> Love anything and your heart will certainly be wrung and possibly broken. If you want to make sure of keeping it intact, you must give your heart to no-one, not even to an animal. Wrap it up carefully round with hobbies and little luxuries, avoid all entanglements, lock it up safe in the casket or coffin of your selfishness. But in that casket – safe, dark, motionless, airless – it will change. It will not be broken, it will become unbreakable, impenetrable, irredeemable. The alternative to tragedy or at least the risk of tragedy, is damnation. The only place outside Heaven where you can be perfectly safe from all the dangers of

perturbations of love is Hell. I believe that the most law-less and inordinate loves are less contrary to God's will than a self-invited and self-protective lovelessness.[*]

The words 'unbreakable, impenetrable, irredeemable' express well the position of the ego that, through pride, locks itself into itself.

Both these scenarios result in a terrible state of isolation, in a person who is strong, self-contained, unable to be hurt and immune from emotional entanglements. It is a secure place where the only person that can be depended or relied upon is oneself. It is exceptionally difficult to break out of this position which feels to the individual locked into it extremely attractive and secure.

There are only two possible ways out of this situation and neither is really in the control of the person who has become entrapped. Both alternatives are unlikely but this is not to say that they are impossible:

1. Sometimes an individual will meet a person who loves him or her enough to accept and cope with the rejection, the defences and the hurt that the person will inflict as a means to the self-preservation of his or her own ego. The ego will not, out of pride, give in without a very hard fight and it will test the love being offered to breaking point. Love is seen by the ego as a threat because it requires the ego to be dethroned, and this is the one thing that it cannot accept. Once an ego has reached this point, then it will treat any love with suspicion; it will reject, test and attempt to destroy it or at least to undermine it. The ego is always looking for the opportunity to be able to tell itself, 'I told you so. I was right to keep up the barriers. All relationships fail and there is no point to any of them.' Such is the ego's desire to reinforce the image the ego has created that it will do all it can to torpedo the love it is encountering from the person who is prepared to love him or her despite knowing how thoroughly unlovable he or she is. It is highly unlikely that anyone will love another sufficiently to be able to

---

[*] C. S. Lewis. in chapter six of *The Four Loves* (London, Fount, 1998).

take this sort of continued rejection and in the end he or she will simply walk away – which, of course, enables the ego to tell itself, 'I told you so'! Sometimes a man (it is usually a man) will lash out if he is loved – either physically or emotionally. This happens when the love starts to break down the barriers his self has constructed and violence of some sort seems the only way to repulse the threat that the love represents to the constructed self. Strangely, and yet understandably, love can be the cause of the violence precisely because it is seen as a threat. It is only if love can penetrate the barriers and resistance that there remains any hope that the person locked into ego may be rescued.

2. The second alternative is for a person to reach the stage where life is so appalling, so meaningless and pointless that everything seems futile, everything seems hopeless. In this extreme state of despair or depression life itself seems devoid of value or meaning, every possible way forward seems a dead end, love is a forgotten dream to be regarded with cynicism, and death begins to appear an attractive release. Strangely, it is precisely reaching this point of despair which may, as we shall see in a later chapter, provide grounds for hope – but this is a terrible position for a person to find him or herself in, and finding a way forward is by no means certain.

Despair lurks beneath the surface of the lives of all individuals whose centre is themselves although they may well not recognise it – indeed, they will be unable to recognise it but that does not mean that it is not a reality. No matter how the ego is fed, no matter what pleasures it uses to build itself up, no matter how great the appeal of the pursuits that it chooses, they all eventually fail to fulfil and to satisfy. This sounds depressing because it is!

Even if people can manage to convince themselves that the life that is self-centred has meaning and value, the security they have constructed for themselves begins to disintegrate in the face of the growing proximity of death. Whether their ego is based on money, reputation, possessions, pleasure, hobbies, relationship or family, it is undermined the nearer death comes and the underlying despair becomes harder to suppress. Most people, however, do not like to dwell on this and instead keep themselves occupied and busy as long as they possibly can. This is well put by a story retold by Tolstoy in his *Confessions*:

An old Eastern fable tells of a traveller who is surprised by a ferocious wild animal. To escape, the traveller hides in an empty well, but at the bottom of the well he sees a dragon with its jaws open, ready to devour him. He does not dare to climb out because he is afraid of being eaten by the hungry beast, nor does he dare drop to the bottom of the well for fear of being eaten by the dragon. He seizes hold of a branch of a bush that is growing in the crevices of the well and clings to it. His arms grow weak and he knows he will soon have to resign himself to the death that awaits him on either side. Yet he still clings on, and while he is holding onto the branch he looks around and sees that two mice, one black and one white, are steadily working their way round the bush he is hanging from, gnawing away at it. Sooner or later they will eat through it and the branch will snap, and he will fall into the jaws of the dragon. The traveller sees this and knows that he will inevitably perish. While he is still hanging there he sees some drops of honey on the leaves of the bush, he stretches out his tongue and licks them.

In the same way I am clinging to the tree of life, knowing that the dragon of death awaits me, and I cannot understand how I have fallen into this torment. I try licking the honey that once consoled me, but it no longer gives me pleasure. The white mouse and the black mouse – day and night – are gnawing at the branch from which I am hanging. I can see the dragon clearly and the honey no longer tastes sweet. I can only see one thing; the inescapable dragon and the mice, and I cannot tear my eyes away from them, and this is no fable but the truth, the truth that is irrefutable and intelligible to everyone.

The ability of Western society to marginalise death is one of its most impressive feats. Many people never encounter death, never see a dead body – death is sanitised and pushed to the margins so that it does not have to be confronted.

Once human beings acknowledge death, they are forced to look at themselves again. This may happen at various stages in life, and at such 'turning points' individuals may require counselling or therapy to enable them to live through them and to move forward. Yet there is a significant danger that some counsellors merely seek to help individuals to construct a new picture of reality by which they can live, so enabling them to re-enthrone the ego at the centre of their existence. This is likely to make them happy and enable them to cope again, but they are happy because their ego is back in control – they are enabled once more to see themselves as worthwhile and significant and this is what they desire more than anything else. Counselling can some-times, with the best of intentions, reconstruct a new picture of reality which reinforces the idea that 'I'm OK!' The only trouble is that this may well be a false picture which will only break down when another critical period in the individual's life is reached.

The Implications for Ethics

If the centre of a person's life is him or herself, then ethics becomes entirely a matter of what will suit the individual best. There are no absolutes: the only relevant criterion will be per-sonal decision-making based on self-interest. To be sure, there may still be ethical reflection, but it will be based on the issue of how any decision will affect the person concerned. In the short term, such people may act in ways that run counter to their immediate interests – but they will only do so because they consider that in this way their own longer-term interests are likely to be prospered.

A few examples might illustrate the different ways in which this could happen:

A member of a company whose chairperson is a conservative politician and who is seeking advancement might express strong views against drugs and against immigration, in favour of lower taxes and 'family values', but these attitudes may be motivated by the desire to please the chairperson in order to keep open the possibility of advancement in the company.

A member of the teaching staff at a United States' university might consider the novels of a modern black feminist to be poorly written and to lack substance, but in order to fit in, to look good amidst colleagues and students, and not to become vulnerable to attacks by a powerful feminist lobby which could affect promotion prospects, he might consider it essential to portray himself as an avid reader.

On finding herself unexpectedly pregnant, a woman who has not reflected on ethical issues might consider that the right moral choice is 'obviously' to abort the child, since otherwise her life plan would be threatened. Lacking any independent way of questioning or validating her decision the only issue which motivates her might be what is convenient to her.

On discovering that a close family member has been raped, is pregnant and has decided on an abortion, a prominent member of the local Catholic Church community might take a very strong anti-abortion stance fully aware that this might mean being alienated from his family. If the person's centre is himself, his real aim in making a strong moral stand might be to increase his standing in his community (there is no necessity here and other motivations might obviously be possible).

The point that should be clear from these brief examples is that often moral decision making is not made on the basis of a dispassionate assessment of what is right or wrong, but rather on self-interest – cunningly concealed, of course, beneath layers of respectability. Frequently it is exceptionally hard to work out a person's real motives and even the individuals concerned find it hard to know what the real reasons for their actions are. Sometimes, however, the position is clearer and some people will openly take decisions solely on the basis of self-interest – for instance, in the sexual sphere making decisions based on what will suit their own interests or what will bring them pleasure, with no thought for any others involved.

The motto of the devil is held to be '"Do what you will" shall be the whole of the law'. This sums up the view of those who live for self. If self is really at the centre of these individuals' lives (way down, of course, beneath the surface layers of those things which people tell themselves are at the centre!) then 'Do what you will' is their real motto. The only constraint on their behaviour may be the communities in which they live. Acting in anti-social ways may cause them pain and, therefore, choosing to conform rather than to stand out from the crowd will ultimately lead to greater satisfaction. This is ethical egoism at work – making decisions based solely on the interests of the individual.

If self is at the centre, the interests of others are irrelevant. Individuals fail to see others as people to be valued and respected but see them instead in purely instrumental terms – as means to the end of their own pleasure or self-satisfaction. It cannot, however, be emphasised strongly enough that 'pleasure' here is not meant in any simple, hedonistic sense. Pleasure may come from enjoying fine art, dining well, attending the theatre, promoting a charity, a church group one cares about, or doing well in business – basically any of these can be primarily hedonistic. The key point for all those who live for self is that beneath these apparent aims is a deeper and more profound reality – concern with self alone.

The last chapter argued that those without a centre have no core to their lives, nothing for which they would live or die or which can provide the fulcrum for their existence. They therefore fail to fulfil their human potential and are in much the same state as animals who are dominated by the moment and what is of passing attraction. Such a life will almost certainly lead to despair whether or not it is recognised (and it may not be). This chapter has argued that even those who have carefully considered the options and who do have a genuine psychological centre – themselves – are also subject to despair because of the unsatisfactory nature of their existence and because they have no basis for ethical reflection on the problems of today. They, too, fail to fulfil their human potential. Since much of the world's population may fall into one or other of these two groups (although, since there is no way of measuring this, modern empirically based psychology ignores it), it is not surprising that we are in a moral mess.

However, self is not the only possible centre for a person's life.

Some people are reflective and realise the need for a centre for their lives that does not depend on ego. These individuals may have an ethical centre. It is to them that we turn our attention in the next chapter.

9

Living for Ethics

The title of this chapter appears strange. What might it mean to 'live for ethics' or to have an ethically centred life?

Chapter seven argued that the lives of many people are devoid of a psychological centre; they are blown this way and that by peer group pressure, by media influence or by the latest opinions of the day. These people have no ground on which ethical reflection can be based and therefore fail to realise their human potential.

In chapter eight it was argued that those whose centre is themselves anchor their lives solely on what they want or on what will boost their ego. They will choose actions which reinforce the dominance of their own self. Pride reinforces this constructed self but beneath it lurks despair which, when it allows itself to be confronted by reality, knows that what has been constructed is meaningless and empty. However, these considerations are generally suppressed and life continues to be busy, active and, apparently, happy.

However, there is a much rarer group of people who choose another centre to their lives. Instead of choosing themselves as the centre they choose to live by an ethical standard or an ethical system that they have appropriated and made their own. They choose – deliberately and clearly – a centre which will provide the pivot and fulcrum for their lives. They choose to create a self using ethics as their centre.

For such a person, becoming a self is still central, as it must be for anyone who wants to become fully human.* However,

---

* This is an important point that will be developed later. Aristotle

instead of choosing the route to selfhood through self-centredness, such a person makes a mature, thoughtful ethical choice and seeks identity in the act of choice. The choice, once made, is final and identity is found by living through that choice, by being faithful to it and maintaining fidelity to it through all that transpires.

There are many different theories of ethics but, in a sense, they all miss the point. This is a large claim and one which needs justification. Philosophers debate ethical theories and devise arguments which either explain what does happen in terms of moral decision making or what they consider should happen. Philosophy students in universities study different ethical systems and pursue their intricacies, their strengths and weaknesses. There are many ethical theories which are studied assiduously and in detail. However, the study of ethics does not necessarily make a person more ethical – it is easy to study a subject academically but for it to have no impact on one's life.

It is rare to find anyone living in the normal world (or in any sphere of life for that matter) who actually lives according to any of the ethical theories that have been developed. It simply does not work like that. In fact, many people who are regarded as profoundly good, moral individuals have never studied ethics at all and, if such people are compared, there is found to be no single ethical system that they all adopt. Nelson Mandela, Martin Luther King, Mother Teresa, Simone Weil, Vaclav Havel, the Buddha, Jesus of Nazareth, St Francis of Assisi, Florence Nightingale, and many others would be hailed as good people by all those who knew about their lives, but there is no ethical system that unites them (although they all shared a belief in an objective moral order – they would all have found post-modernism incredible). The lack of a single ethical system which unites them should make one cautious in thinking that to be ethical means to embrace a particular ethical system or ideal.

---

considered that a human being – and every other living thing – can be defined in terms of potentialities. These potentialities are not exhausted just by natural growth and reaching adulthood – they extend beyond this to the sort of person one is to become. See chapter three.

Plato was a profoundly good person, admired by all who knew him – and so was Aristotle, his one-time pupil. Yet Aristotle rejected almost all of Plato's philosophy. It was not ethical theory that made Aristotle and Plato who they were. Certainly they were brilliant philosophers and between them they provided the foundation for Western philosophy, but they were also more than that. They were good human beings who influenced others by who they were as much as by what they taught and wrote.

It is the activity of a lifetime to study the complex web of ethical reflection which human beings have inherited. To become an academic philosopher specialising in ethics takes many, many years and even after prolonged study he or she will be an expert in only one relatively small area of knowledge. No one can be an expert on all Western ethical theories – and even professional Western ethicists rarely have any real grasp of Eastern ethical theories. It simply is not possible to acquire comprehensive knowledge of all ethical theories and, even if this knowledge were acquired, it would not resolve the challenges of postmodernism.

The choice of an ethically centred life

If, then, forming a self by centring one's life on ethics does not involve rationally thinking through and adopting a particular ethical system, what does it involve? Essentially it involves choice – making choices and then being willing to live consistently by these choices. Choice here represents an active decision: it is a core commitment that provides a framework for life. It is not something that can simply happen without being noticed. It means a thoughtful, reflective decision to choose to make an ethical commitment and to hold this at the centre of one's life. The choice may be of many different types and does not need to be singular:

1. It can involve choosing for oneself the ethical system within which one has been brought up, but making it one's own in a deliberate act of free choice. People cannot, of course, control as children the ethical system within which they individually develop, but as they become adults they can choose to

internalise the system and to adopt it for themselves. This is what is meant by making it one's own. For instance, religious believers who are brought up within an ethical framework which as young people they take for granted may, on attaining maturity, study and decide to appropriate it by an act of will (or, of course, they may also choose to reject it – but for the purpose of understanding an ethically committed life we are considering those who make a core commitment to a framework).

2. It can involve choosing an alternative system to that with which one is familiar – possibly after a period of study or by coming into contact with people who impress and who live by this system. This is the route of conversion (possibly, but not necessarily, represented by a religious conversion) where a free choice is made to adopt an alternative framework which may be at variance to that of one's family and peers.

3. It can involve making a more practical choice such as the decision to get married, to commit to a partner or even to take a vow of celibacy and then to live one's life, without compromise, by being faithful to this decision.

4. It can involve coming to a realisation that one's actions have led one to become the sort of person that one does not wish to be and resolving, as a result, to bring about a change and to commit to a new, ethical approach to life which will provide a ground or framework for all one does.

In all these cases, however, the choice is not a whim, not a matter of feeling, not a passing fad. Instead, it involves making a rational choice, a core commitment which thereafter will regulate, frame and control everything that a person does. This will then provide the centre for the whole of his or her life. There is a real sense in which a person who takes this step creates him or herself by the choice that is made. The choice represents a commitment to something which is placed at the centre of who the person is. Betraying this would then become a matter of betraying oneself – it would mean abandoning the commitment so that the choice no longer has significance and becomes no more than a whim or passing fancy. In making a choice, one commits oneself to the choice and makes oneself responsible for it – indeed, being responsible is a central part of the ethical life. This is why the freedom to choose and choice itself is of such importance as it involves a commitment that is not conditional, that is not going to be abandoned because things do not work out as anticipated. The choice is, from this point of view, decisive. It involves a person making a choice to put something other than him or herself at the centre of his or her life.

The binding nature of ethical choice

Those who place self at the centre regard so-called commitments like marriage, in which vows or promises are made, as no more than temporary expedients which can be abandoned when they are no longer convenient. This is exactly the reverse of an ethical choice. The whole point about an ethical choice is that it provides a fixed point, a fulcrum around which a person's self-identity is constructed and for which he or she is then responsible.

In deciding to get married, individuals make a choice, they commit. In the words of the marriage service each partner commits to the other 'for better or worse, for richer for poorer, in sickness and health until death do us part'. This is a good example of ethical choice: it is intended as a permanent, binding commitment which will endure in all circumstances and is not conditional. It does not depend on being loved in return, on feelings remaining the same, on not getting bored, or on appearance. It is a freely entered into, binding and irrevocable commitment, at least it is if it is an ethical choice. Having made the choice, the process then begins of a person forming him or herself according to this choice, literally creating him or herself, by being loyal to, living out and being responsible for the choice. Everything else is relative to the choice that is made and is thus subservient to it.

Such a way of looking at ethical choice is a rarity today. Permanent binding marriage (or other) vows are becoming increasingly unusual. Certainly the words are said and probably at the time they are meant, but subconsciously limitations are placed. In many countries prenuptial agreements are now made so that if the marriage breaks up, financial matters are dealt with.

Even if this is not done, legal frameworks exist for the distribution of property on divorce. However, this way of thinking is precisely a denial of the ethical choice that gives marriage its validity. The old marriage service said 'With all my worldly goods I thee endow' – modern marriages effectively add the words 'subject to our prenuptial agreements or to the fair distribution of goods if the marriage fails taking into account what we brought into the marriage'. Once vows are made with get-out clauses or even with the possibility that the marriage will fail and the vows will be renounced, then the vows are not being made from an ethical perspective but from a selfish perspective in which a person is really saying, 'I promise to be faithful to this marriage as long as it suits me'. In this case, the message is very clear. It is not ethics but self-interest that is in the driving seat.

No one enters marriage thinking that it is going to fail, the presupposition is that it will succeed. Nevertheless, at the back of the new husband's or wife's mind may well be the prudential calculation, 'If it fails, then ...'. In this 'if' hisses the voice of self-interest, the voice of caution and the clear indication that it is not an ethical commitment that is being made.

An ethical choice is of an entirely different order – it is a choice which is then used to provide a framework and determinant for all other choices. It does not depend on contingent matters and eventualities, rather contingent matters and eventualities depend on it. This is the point about the nature of marriage promises – they are meant to be unconditional, to be independent of the way things turn out. Irrespective of economic circumstance, health factors or any other contingencies, the promises are meant to hold firm. This is the nature of an ethical choice. In choosing to marry, a person is deciding on a fixed point for his or her life which will determine all other points. The fact that most people today do not look at marriage promises in these terms precisely shows that they are not ethically centred individuals. The vows they make are either a matter of convention, emotional feeling, convenience or whim and thus can be discarded comparatively lightly, or they are expressions of self-interest and thus can be discarded once the self decides that it is no longer in its interests to keep them.

The failure rate of first marriages in the Western world is in excess of 40 per cent whilst the failure rate of second marriages is considerably above 50 per cent. The higher rate of failure for second marriages is not surprising, as the failure of the first marriage represents an acceptance that the first commitment was a contingent one based on self-interest or convention. The ethical significance of the marriage vows has already been overcome by the ego. Instead of being an absolute to which husbands and wives hold themselves responsible and by which their very self is formed, the commitment becomes disposable, relative to the situation in which they find themselves. Once people embark on the path of making commitments and choices mere matters of convenience, then they demonstrate their understanding of choice and commitment is selfish and self-centred. The prospect that this approach might change when a second set of choices are made is very low indeed – unless, and this is rare, there is a radical change in the person making them. Of course, he or she intends to keep the second set of vows, just as he or she meant to keep the first set but, effectively, the choices that are being made are essentially self-centred and it is only if the self making the choices becomes an entirely different self that the outcome can be expected to be different.

An example of such a turning point is presented in Henrik Ibsen's play *A Doll's House*. The heroine of the play, Nora, decides to leave her husband, Thorvald, when she comes to realise that she has been playing the part of a doll wife just as she had previously played the part of a doll daughter to her father. Both the significant men in her life were happy to treat her as if she were a doll, a plaything. They want her to conform, to perform tricks to please them, and to comply with their ideas of what a daughter and a wife should be. Neither of them considers who Nora is as an individual, a person. When she announces her decision to leave, Thorvald is appalled and confronts her with her ethical duty. What are the guiding principles of her life? What about her religion? Nora is confronted with a turning point – for the first time she is thinking for herself, she is responsible for herself and not just acting in her role as daughter or wife. She has moved from being a child to being a responsible adult. She says she has no idea about such matters at all. All she knows is what the pastor and others have told her but she has never really thought these things through for herself before. She has to leave Thorvald in order to start thinking about whether what the pastor said was right, or at least right *for her*. She clearly recognises that she has not internalised the ethical system in which she had been living. It was like a comfortable old coat, but she never made it her coat. She has grown up and come to recognise that grown-ups make decisions for themselves.

As Nora puts her on her cloak and is about to leave, Thorvald pleads with her to stay and look after the children. Nora says that she is most certainly not the person to bring up the children, she needs to bring herself up first. She does not know who she is, so how can she bring up her children? However, she is determined to find out, and that is why she needs to leave. Thorvald finally asks if there is not any hope for the two of them to remain together. Nora replies that for there to be hope, 'the greatest miracle in the world would have to take place'. Thorvald, thoroughly annoyed by this time, asks what this 'greatest miracle' might be. She replies that this greatest miracle would be if they could both so change that what they had could become a marriage. Her point is very clear. Neither of them have been selves. They have been playing at being married, playing at their roles, but neither was a self. Neither really loved and neither was really competent to enter into a true marriage. Nora leaves and Thorvald is left alone, without really understanding what has happened except that Nora has left him. Nora, by contrast, has understood the situation and has woken up to the need for change. This process of 'waking up' is a vital precursor to the ethical stage.

The Buddha, after his enlightenment, was asked, 'Are you a God, are you a saint?' He replied, 'No, I am awake.' When Nora awoke to her condition, it was the first step in seeking to become a self. The ethical person, then, is the person who does not drift but makes core commitments which provide the bedrock within which his or her self is constructed.

Ethical choice resting on human institutions

In philosophy it was Immanuel Kant who most clearly expressed this idea of acting rationally from a sense of duty and seeking to develop a 'good will' – namely a will that always acted out of duty. For him, reason was indeed supreme and the strength of personal will that commanded human beings always to do their duty irrespective of consequences was fearsome. Kant considered that everyone should seek the *summum bonum* – the coincidence of virtue and happiness – and believed that if people would only act according to reason then happiness would be achieved, if not in this life then in the next.

It is important to recognise that the ethical life as set out here is not connected to God, even if a person may consider the ethical framework they adopt to be given by God. Kant's ethics did not depend on God but on reason, and even the claim that one's ethics are God-given becomes suspect on careful analysis, as will be made clear shortly. *The ethical life sees no appeal beyond the chosen ethical system. The ethical system that has been chosen is the central, immovable point for the individual and there is no appeal beyond this. This is a crucial point, the significance of which will emerge later.*

Those who centre their lives on an ethical choice will be rare and strong individuals and may well be considered worthy of admiration. They will be trustworthy, honest, consistent, reliable, keep their word, keep secrets, be predictable and live a good life. Morality is meant to be, and is, praiseworthy. The ethical individual should be a good and happy individual. For such individuals, reason is likely to reign supreme – they will have considered the alternatives, rationally assessed and thought through the choices they have made, and committed themselves to them. They will be responsible for their choices and will act out of a sense of duty.

Sadly, however, the ethically centred life is also likely to end in despair, which in a way seems most lamentable. It represents such a noble and strong commitment, it requires so much conviction to live it through, it is so rare and it seems so admirable that surely it deserves a happy outcome. However, life is not like that. At the end of the day the person who lives ethically may come to realise (although they will almost certainly seek to disguise this fact from themselves) that their sense of duty, their sense of responsibility, indeed the whole ethical life that they are living rests on choices that they themselves have made. In effect, therefore, they are living by relation to a construct in the same way as those whose lives are centred on their ego. To be sure, great strength of will is required to maintain fidelity to the ethical choices and commitments which the construct represents, but even this strength constantly breaks down in the face of circumstance. It breaks down even more with the realisation that the driving force of duty rests merely on something that has been created by one's own supposedly free choice. The result is that this choice is almost impossible to maintain and the ethically centred person then feels a failure. It simply is not possible to maintain loyalty to an ethical system and, even if one succeeds, by tremendous effort, one is forced to recognise that what is being related to is merely one's own construction, the product of one's own choice. Both possibilities lead to despair.

Both Jesus and St Paul recognised this. Jesus saw that the Jewish law had become so onerous and detailed that it had become an end in itself rather than a means to an end. Many of the Jews of Jesus' time were, of course, sure that the Torah provided the detailed law by which they lived and was God-given in its every detail. Jesus rejected this, and he himself laid down no ethical system. The spirit that lay beneath the Torah, which guided and inspired the old law, had been destroyed by legalism. Jesus himself constantly broke the rules of the society in which he lived and, as a result, was strongly disapproved of by the supposedly pious and respectable members of society. St Paul saw that obedience to the Jewish law was a form of slavery which could not bring human wholeness.* The more people

---

* St Paul was remarkably rude to the Jewish community who had not become Christians likening them to slaves (to the law). They were, he said, the real children of the slave girl Hagar whom Abraham slept with to produce Ishmael, whilst Christians were the real children of the free woman, Sarah. It is difficult to overestimate the offence this would have given to the Jewish community who prided themselves on being the children of Abraham via his son, Isaac.

sought to keep the law, the clearer it became how far away they were from achieving their aim, and this brought despair. Being virtuous by an act of will is a fine ideal, but only those who have attempted it know how far short they constantly fall and how impossible it is to attain.

It may, of course, be argued that relating wholly to an ethical commitment does not depend on choice but on some absolute system of ethics or the commands of God. However, there are very real problems to this view. So much depends on the community within which one is brought up and its values. The ethical system to which people relate is strongly dependent on conformity to the community of which they form a part. In this case what people have at the centre of their lives is merely what they have absorbed from the culture into which they were born. A few lines attributed to Abraham Lincoln put this well:

If you were born where they were born
And you were taught what they were taught,
You would believe what they believe.

Members of every culture naturally consider that it is *their* culture which has the only right values and that all others are inferior – this is part of the normal belief pattern of every framework. Therefore:

- a person born in Tehran will be a Muslim
- a person born in Greece will be Greek Orthodox
- a person born in Leningrad in the sixties would have been a communist
- a person born in Tibet prior to the Chinese invasion, would have been a Buddhist
- a person born in parts of the Southern United States would be a Baptist
- a person born in Ireland would be a Catholic.

Of course, there are exceptions to these generalisations, but nevertheless most of us are 'formed' into the tradition of our parents, our schools and our community unless, of course, we reject these altogether and decide to place self at the centre and to go our own way. Religious congregations and religious orders talk of 'formation' – forming people into the culture and belief systems of which they have agreed to be a part. The same applies to a humanist or atheistic framework, which again requires formation. Most of us are educated into a moral framework which we then more or less accept. Making an ethical choice, however, goes beyond this: individuals choose to internalise a framework, making it their own so that their whole identity depends on their commitment to it. This may seem to be arguing that all morality is relative to the community in which a person lives and it may seem to the reader that what is being maintained here is a relativist, antirealist or postmodern view. This is not, however, the case. The reason why requires explanation, which will be given in chapter twelve.

Unless people personally commit themselves to a psychological centre for their lives, the framework they choose – whether it be the one in which they have grown up or not – will not have real ethical significance. They will inhabit the framework as long as it suits them but quietly abandon it when it is no longer convenient. This is not an ethical stance. A freely chosen, self-aware commitment is a necessary part of an ethical life.

This leaves open the question whether there is any single or absolute ethical system, but the crucial point is not whether the ethical system individuals adopt is the 'most right' or the 'only right' one (they will almost always consider that this is the case with the system they have chosen) but whether they have chosen to appropriate it and to centre the whole of their existence on it. Only if this is done can the truth beneath that system begin to emerge, only then will it become true for the individual who has adopted it.

This is why detached philosophical arguments about the rights and wrongs of alternative ethical systems are of so little relevance. The problem is precisely that these arguments are detached. Wisdom was never found nor truth discovered in the ethical or religious spheres by detachment. It is only the person who is passionately committed to the choice that is made who can begin to emerge as an individual, as a self, and can begin to find a subjective truth for which he or she can live and, if necessary, die.

Amnesty International chronicles the huge range of people who have, as individuals, stood up against the power of the state and have been imprisoned, tortured and marginalised as a result. However, it is always individuals who take these stands, and this is because such action requires individual decision, albeit it is normally one that entails deciding to conform to a certain ethical view adhered to by the group to which he or she happens to belong.

Passionate, personal engagement is central to becoming a self, and cautious, rational indifference is precisely the enemy of self-hood. Yet few people are passionate. For more and more people in the Western world, life is comfortable with little in the way of real challenge. There is never any need to place self on the line, to make a stand or to be passionate about what one believes. The result is a grey conformity influenced by the media and peer groups which has little to do with an ethical outlook on life. Unless a person is concerned passionately with the question 'Who am I?', unless they genuinely seek to form a self, then ethical issues will not have any real meaning for them. Of course, those whose have an ethical centre will have this concern, but as we have seen, this will not prevent despair occurring when they come to realise that they cannot succeed in living the ethical life by seeking to comply with the ideals they have chosen or created.

Community is vital to ethics. A community of agreed values and conventions provides the milieu within which ethical life is lived. However, it is precisely here that tension arises. Once the standards of the group or society are allowed to become the determining factor in deciding how to live, individuality can be undermined even if a person has made a commitment to live by these standards. There is no appeal beyond these agreed standards and they provide the final arbiter of right and wrong for those who adhere to them.

Society has many effective ways of demanding obedience to its shared values:

1. Economic success, even at the level of buying a house and maintaining a job, may demand compliance with the ethical values of the organisation and society within which a person lives and works. Standing out against these values will result

in sanctions which seem intolerable, particularly for those who have dependants.

2. Society – and, indeed, ethics – demands total disclosure by individuals, requiring that they have no secrets. Ethics involves disclosure. It demands that all actions should be taken in the open and that the routines of society governing marriage, birth, death and social interaction should be maintained. Society rewards disclosure and punishes secrecy, considering that the latter means living for self and not the community. Thus adultery, theft, lying or refusing to work may all, perfectly reasonably, be considered anti-social behaviour and condemned. The point here is not, however, about whether this condemnation is right or wrong but about the resultant pressure on every individual to conform to the ethical thinking of the rest of society. This then means that the final arbiter of ethical rightness or wrongness becomes the community or society.

3. Wider interests are almost always ignored by ethical systems within particular societies and global issues affecting other societies are not dealt with. There are many examples of this, including the fate of AIDS victims in Africa, the global inequalities resulting from world trade and globalisation, child labour, endemic racism and wars in much of the world, the suffering of animals, and the power of multi-nationals. Once community becomes the determinant of ethics, then these uncomfortable issues can be sidetracked, marginalised and ignored. Of course, there are charities that do a certain amount in these areas, but the ethics of every group tends to favour itself and does not recognise the radical equality of all human beings which may necessitate more drastic action in changing institutions and systems so that institutional evil is not perpetuated. Indeed, the prevalence of institutional evil[*] may be the greatest area that commitment to an ethical system fails to address as often ethics precisely derives from the

---

[*] The issue of institutional evil is dealt with in more detail in *The Thinkers' Guide to Evil* by Peter Vardy and Julie Arliss (Alresford, John Hunt Publishing, 2003).

institutions or communities in which a person lives (whether this is country, religious or corporate organisation or family). *The ethical life does not have within it the capacity to challenge the ethical system which shapes it.*

4. Catholic social ethics has a rich and important field of reflection centred on the idea of 'the common good' – effectively this sets out a demand to work for and foster the common good rather than one's own, selfish, good. This is combined with the work of charities such as CAFOD, which work to bring some relief to the third world. This commitment to the common good is admirable, but the problem immediately arises as to how one defines the word 'common'. In practice it tends to be defined in terms of one's own community and is extended only as far as those with whom a particular community identifies closely. It very rarely extends, for instance, to the third world. The medical budget in Africa is measured in terms of a few dollars per head per year, yet few argue that what is regarded as an acceptable level of health care in Europe or America should be extended to Africa as the 'common' in the phrase 'common good' is too narrowly defined. Societies tend to be self-interested and to focus on their own needs with little regard for wider interests. The United Nations requested rich countries, twenty years ago, to give one per cent of their GDP to the third world but the amount being given is falling ever further below this figure. Few protest because the 'common good' does not extend beyond their own communities.

The ethical life, as described in this chapter, may well be lived by someone with religious convictions. Thus Buddhists, Christians, Jews and Muslims all have their own ethical systems and many religious people consider 'being religious' to involve commitment to these systems. This commitment will be passionate and deep (at least if the individual lives the ethical life) but what makes it ethical rather than religious is that the commitment is to the system of ethics and not to any notion of a transcendent 'other' (except, of course, that many will say that their particular system has been laid down by this 'other' which some call God).

Living for ethics, then, demands a choice, a commitment, and an acceptance of the permanent obligations that this commitment entails. Nevertheless, these commitments are still strongly culturally relative and will be almost impossible to live up to. Both these factors contribute to despair.

The Implications for Ethics

If becoming fully human extends beyond a physical description of a human being, then the psychological centre of individuals must be taken seriously. Chapter seven argued that most people have no centre to their lives at all; they simply conform to the society in which they live, with that community and the media playing a crucial role in the formation of their views. Such people do not think outside the bounds laid down by their cultural milieu and have no real centre to their lives other than that culture. They are like a drunken man in a wagon, pulled by a horse that has no idea where it is going.

Then there are those, described in chapter eight, who are in control of the wagon that is their self. They drive it where they wish to go and the sole determinant of their actions is they themselves. Mozart's Don Giovanni or Goethe's Faust are good examples of such individuals.

In this chapter the position of a third group has been outlined representing those who are in control of the wagon and drive it according to a decision or decisions which they have made. This group of people live for ethics, and it is on these ethics that they base the choices they make. These people 'create themselves' through their commitments and their fidelity to these commitments. They may either make a conscious, self-aware choice to follow the ethical system of the community of which they are a part, or more specific choices such as to undertake the commitment involved in marriage. These individuals allow their ethical choices to determine the way things go, rather than allowing the way things go to determine their ethical choices. They are clearly highly motivated individuals who may well be quietly proud of the depth of their reflection and their achievement in being faithful to their commitments. They will have a strong sense of individual responsibility and will be willing to sacrifice everything for the choices they have made. Nevertheless behind this strong and sometimes proud exterior – for there is much about which the ethical individual can rightly be proud – there will nevertheless lurk despair as adherence to an ethical system cannot provide meaning nor can anyone actually live up to the demands of ethics (as Jesus and St Paul both recognised).

People in this group have a rational basis for ethical reflection based on the framework of choices they have made. They will, therefore, use reason to try to determine the correct way to behave in the concrete situation in which they find themselves, but reason will always be applied within the framework they have chosen. Some examples may illustrate this.

An ethical man chooses to marry on the basis of a mature ethical decision. Marriage provides a framework assumption within which he develops as a self; it is a core commitment. Over the years he finds his love has died, but nevertheless he remains faithful to the commitment he has made. His wife may then have one or more affairs and may make it clear that she does not love him any more – still his original commitment to the marriage will be unswerving. His wife may eventually choose to leave him and demand financial support, but he will still remain faithful to his promises. Even when his wife finally divorces him and marries another man, he will still be obedient to the ethical choice he has made. He promised 'till death do us part' and although she may have divorced him he will never remarry or live with another woman. His marriage vow will always remain in effect and will always be binding – it in no way depends on his wife's actions. He has made a core commitment and will remain unswervingly true to this, thus preserving his own integrity and identity as a person.

An adherent to a particular philosophic view of ethics (although these are, as we have already seen, rare in terms of actually living in accordance with a philosophic system) will conduct their ethical reflection within the framework provided by the system. Thus, a utilitarian will seek to maximise happiness and will use this as a basis for making moral decisions. The idea that there could be acts that are wrong on non-utilitarian grounds will not arise as their framework rules this out.

A traditional Catholic who has made the choice to be faithful to the teachings of the Catholic Magisterium, will accept its teaching that, for example, life begins at conception, even though there is no way of proving it. All ethical reflection on, for instance, abortion, IVF, pre-implantation genetic diagnosis, stem cell research, etc., will take place within this framework. This basic assumption will not be challenged and ethical discussion will take place within these parameters.

A communist philosopher who had chosen to appropriate and adopt the communist credo under the old USSR would only be willing to see and discuss political theory in terms of class struggle. Any other way of seeing the world would simply be unacceptable. Similarly for young Maoists who had chosen to conform to the teachings they had been given at the time of the Cultural Revolution in China, Mao Zedong's *Little Red Book* was inspired and was to be taken literally as truth and used to regulate the conduct of society and all matters of ethics.

Many people in the United States consider themselves free and consider themselves to live ethical lives. However, their ethical reflection will generally be developed only within a distinctive 'US' view of the world which is likely to be intolerant of those who are not persuaded of the benefits of capitalism or individual freedom of the sort prized by many Americans and which scarcely comprehends or engages with the perspective of the world's poor or those belonging to fundamentalist Islam or Hinduism.

To a devout Jew, pigs are unclean – they must never be eaten. Even if he or she were to be starving after a plane crash in a remote area of the Andes and the only way to stay alive was to eat a wild pig that had been caught, then there would be no question of doing so. No matter what the consequences, this action would be considered morally wrong. There is a long tradition of this sort of action. At the time of Antiochus Epiphanes in 168 BCE, a concerted attempt was made to enforce Greek culture upon the Jewish people. In particular, all Jews were made to eat pork. The first to refuse was an old, widely respected scribe named Eleazar who went to his death gladly in obedience to the law given to Moses. The following story, from 2 Maccabees 7, is worth retelling in full as it illustrates obedience to an ethical command to an extreme degree:

It also happened that seven brothers with their mother were arrested and tortured with whips and scourges by the king, to force them to eat pork in violation of God's law. One of the brothers, speaking for the others, said: 'What do you expect to achieve by questioning us? We are ready to die rather than transgress the laws of our ancestors.' At that the king, in a fury, gave orders to have pans and cauldrons heated. While they were being quickly heated, he commanded his executioners to cut out the tongue of the one who had spoken for the others, to scalp him and cut off his hands and feet, while the rest of his brothers and his mother looked on. When he was completely maimed but still breathing, the king ordered them to carry him to the fire and fry him. As a cloud of smoke spread from the pan, the brothers and their mother encouraged one another to die bravely, saying such words as these: 'The Lord God is looking on, and he truly has compassion on us, as Moses declared in his canticle, when he protested openly with the words, "And he will have pity on his servants."'

When the first brother had died in this manner, they brought the second to be made sport of. After tearing off the skin and hair of his head, they asked him: 'Will you eat the pork rather than have your body tortured limb by limb?'

Answering in the language of his forefathers, he said, 'Never!' So he too in turn suffered the same tortures as the first. At the point of death he said: 'You accursed fiend, you are depriving us of this present life, but the King of the world will raise us up to live again forever. It is for his laws that we are dying.'

Each of the brothers in turn is treated in the same way with their mother encouraging them to be faithful through the tortures. Finally only the seventh son is left alive. The king appeals to him to eat pork, promising to reward him and to give him high office. He then appeals to the boy's mother to get her final son to save his life but she merely encourages the son to suffer the same fate as his brothers. The youngest son is as steadfast as his older brothers, saying to the King: 'I offer up my body and my life for our ancestral laws, imploring God to show mercy soon to our nation, and by afflictions and blows to make you confess that he alone is God.'

The king, enraged, treated him worse than his brothers and finally killed the mother as well. This terrible story is a good example of a willingness to put obedience to an ethical principle at the centre of one's life and to sacrifice everything else for this. Yet it is clear that not eating pork was a culturally relative command which had decisive ethical significance for the identity and claims to selfhood of one community alone.

Certainly, therefore, someone whose life is centred on ethics will make rational ethical decisions and will take responsibility for these decisions, even if this involves not just personal inconvenience but even in some cases death. However, on examination these ethical decisions will tend to be relative to the communities in which people live and the culture that has informed their choices. Individuals whose lives are centred on ethics are not self-centred, quite the reverse. They are willing to subsume their own desires and whims beneath an ethical commitment into which they have freely entered. The community will be vital in framing these commitments and this insight is a key point in postmodernism's critique of traditional approaches to ethics. Traditional approaches do not, postmodernists maintain, take into account the radically relative perspective of the people making the ethical choices.

It can appear that the ethics by which individuals choose to live are totally subjective, dependent solely on the opinion of the community in which they are formed – a view that relativists, anti-realists and postmodernists would hold. However, although it appears that this chapter is supporting this view, in fact it is not. The key point being made is that individuals who centre their life on ethics are making a choice and the framework for that choice will depend on the community of which they form a part. The source of a community's ethics is a separate issue which will be addressed in due course.

It is now necessary to turn to see whether there are any alternative ways out of the ethical morass in which, in a postmodern world, human beings find themselves.

10

Anguish, Despair and Possibility

Anguish

The last three chapters have made frequent references to despair. Chapter seven argued that many people are not selves at all – they have no centre to their life and are creatures of whim acting in whatever way they feel like acting in the variety of circumstances with which they are confronted. Chapter eight argued that some people do seek to form a self: they live lives that do have a centre, but this centre is themselves. Chapter nine argued that a rare group seeks to form a self by living for some ethical system, by entering into mature, reflective ethical commitments.

All three of these ways of living result, it was argued, in despair. This assertion would be rejected by the majority of people and, therefore, it needs justification. Although it may seem a surprising statement, it emerges from an analysis of the human condition and is closely related to the ethical vacuum with which modern men and women find themselves confronted. However, this state of despair can be positive. In chapter eight, the following claim was made:

[One alternative] is for a person to reach the stage where life is so appalling, so meaningless and pointless that everything seems futile, everything seems hopeless. In this extreme state of despair or depression life itself seems devoid of value or meaning, every possible way forward seems a dead end, love is a forgotten dream to be regarded with cynicism, and death begins to appear an attractive release. Strangely, it is precisely reaching this point of despair which may, as we shall see in a later chapter, provide grounds for hope - but this is a terrible position for a person to find him or herself in, and finding a way forward is by no means certain.

A footnote to the passage said that this rather strange claim would be explained in due course – now is the time to attempt this.

If all human beings share a common human nature, then it should be no surprise that their psychological response to existence will be very similar. Individuals have the potential to become fully human, they have the freedom to be able to fully actualise their nature, but it is precisely this freedom that creates anxiety and despair. According to Sartre, all human beings are 'condemned to freedom'.* Individuals have the freedom to choose, but 'we do not choose to be free.'† In other words, the capacity to be free is latent in everyone and it cannot be suppressed but keeps bubbling up – like a spring that one attempts in vain to bury. Individuals have to create who they are but they do not want to take responsibility for doing so. They cannot face being confronted by their freedom so they try to suppress it in order to make themselves forget that it is there. It is this extreme freedom which is central to Sartre's concept of anguish: '. . . freedom, which manifests itself through anguish, is characterised by a constantly renewed obligation to remake the Self which designates the free being.'‡

Individuals cannot avoid being conscious of their freedom, but this knowledge generates anguish about how this freedom will be used. Their anguish leads them to deny that they are free at all because such an awareness would threaten the comfortable, complacent existence most people succeed in forming for themselves. They live in the comfort zone which is precisely the place where freedom is denied. In the comfort zone, there is no

---

* Jean-Paul Sartre, *Being and Nothingness* (London, Methuen, 1966), p. 485.
† *ibid.*, p. 485.
‡ *ibid.*, p. 35.

anguish – precisely because it is comfortable. Reflection on the nature of existence is suppressed as is any reflection about what it is to be a human being. This is one attraction of a life centred on ethics: all those who live ethically have to do is to obey the ethical rules of their community and they will be considered good. However hard this is, it is also straightforward. The guidelines are laid down and are clear. The only problem is to find the strength to follow them.

Anguish arises, however, precisely because life is not that simple and the establishment of sets of rules is not enough to cope with its complexity. Individuals have to decide how to live, how to engage with others and, whilst these ethical rules may help, they are not the final solution.

Anguish is not the same as fear. Fear is an emotion directed at things in the outer world (people are fearful of attack or unemployment or poverty or old age) whereas anguish is felt by individuals about themselves. When we dare to look closely at ourselves, many of us will experience nothingness, emptiness and failure (as the quote from the book of Ecclesiastes on pp. 98–9 makes clear: 'Vanity of vanities, all is vanity'). We cannot bear the thought that our lives are devoid of meaning and purpose. This leads to anguish and dread – we subconsciously realise this and constantly strive to avoid facing it.

Anguish arises when individuals recognise their real state as human beings, and this brings great distress. They experience a vast chasm yawning beneath their feet and they do not know how to respond. It is for this reason that they try to suppress the very thought which gives rise to the anguish – they try to suppress the spring of freedom and to install themselves once more in the comfort zone of security.

Anguish arises when individuals allow themselves to confront themselves. It is reflective. Anguish is always about a person's self; it demands subjectivity and an awareness of self. Unless this is present, anguish will not be experienced. When a person allows themselves to awaken to the freedom they actually have and the decisive effects their free decisions have on themselves, they are left disorientated, with no basis on which to make a decision. They have to let the veils and appearances of their busy day-to-day lives fall away from them as these provide an illusion of purpose. Anguish, then, arises when individuals come to recognise their state. It is thus positive – it is a realisation of where human beings are.

Anguish is generally thought of in negative terms – as something to be avoided and overcome. Who, after all, would choose to be in anguish? If people admit to being in anguish, friends are unlikely to understand and will all too readily dismiss their concerns, emphasising how fortunate they are and how good life is, drawing them back to the comfort zone where all appears to be well. It is painful for a person to remain with their anguish, to consider it and its origins, and such a process will appear to be something to be avoided by any available means.

Anguish arises from the potential an individual has to make choices and despair arises once the person realises who he or she is. It is a mistake to think that this anguish is something to be avoided – quite the reverse. It is a sign that the person is emerging from the veil of illusion into a knowledge of reality. As Sartre says: 'Anguish ... is the recognition of a possibility as my possibility ...'*

Anguish can be positive as it may be the beginning of a reflective and authentic life. It is a sign that human beings are alive and not one of the living dead immersed in the comfort zone of security (which can easily be the security provided by an ethical system) and lack of freedom which often mark an unreflective life. When individuals stop being frightened of the world and their place in it, then anguish and with it a despairing recognition of their state may enter into their consciousness. Only when this happens can the door to meaningful existence be opened.

The overriding human tendency is to do everything possible to avoid anything unpleasant, and certainly anguish falls into this category. People sympathise with those in anguish, they try to 'cheer them up', to be positive about life – in short to drag anyone experiencing anguish down to their own level of unreflective self-awareness. Sartre analyses a series of 'patterns

---

* *ibid.*, p. 34.

of flight' that human beings use to avoid the threat which our realisation of anguish brings. These 'patterns of flight' Sartre calls 'bad faith'. They are attempts at evasion or self-deception.

'Bad faith' is constantly employed by human beings to avoid facing up to their real position by recognising the nothingness and meaninglessness that hide beneath the surface. Human freedom continually reasserts itself and the ego seeks to subdue it. The choices that freedom makes possible are threatening to the ego and to the self that the ego has constructed. People do not like to admit that they are free. Such an admission raises the possibility of them becoming what they are capable of becoming as human beings, and they prefer not to be confronted by this potential.

Despair

Anguish and despair are linked. Anguish arises when human beings comprehend their potential. Once they see that they are not simply glorified animals but that there is a 'more' to being human that every individual can realise, then despair sets in. They realise how far they are from achieving this potential and how impossible the task seems. Despair comes when people are faced by meaninglessness and lack of purpose and see no way forward, no way out. At its most extreme, despair occurs as a result of existing and a person failing even to attempt to realise their true potential. Despair, therefore, comes after anguish – anguish shows the possibilities while despair represents the individual coming to the conclusion that there is no way forward, no way out of their self-created prison.

People can despair over themselves in many different ways. In the initial stages they may feel they are in despair while not actually understanding what has caused it. Kierkegaard put this well when he said:

> Someone in despair despairs over something ... Thus when the power-crazed person whose motto is 'Caesar or nothing' doesn't become Caesar, he despairs over that. But this indicates something else: that he cannot stand being himself precisely because he failed to become Caesar ... to despair over

something is still not really to despair. It is the beginning ...
  A young girl despairs over love, she despairs over losing
the loved one, because he died or became unfaithful. The
despair is not declared. No, she despairs over herself. This
self of hers, which if it had become 'his' beloved she would
have been rid of, or lost, in the most blissful manner – this
self, since it is destined to be a self without 'him' is now an
embarrassment; this self ... has become, now that 'he' is
dead, a loathsome void.*

In this initial stage, despair can be equated with emptiness, a
feeling that nothing matters, particularly material things. Life is
seen as a meaningless vacuum and death can be keenly
anticipated as a welcome release. People in this initial stage may
consider or even attempt suicide because there seems to be no
point to anything – yet this is only a preliminary stage and is not
yet true despair.

A fuller sense of despair is reached when individuals realise
that despair arises not as a result of externals (failing to become
Caesar, losing a boy or girlfriend, or finding life empty and
pointless) but as a result of the person's self. This may be
manifested in various ways.

1. Individuals can fall into despair as a result of turning away
   from freedom and not wanting to be what they are capable of
   being, refusing even to attempt to fulfil their human nature.
   Such individuals have refused the possibilities opened up by
   freedom, denying that they are free and choosing instead to
   see themselves as wholly constrained. They do not want to be
   an individual, a self. They prefer to be just like everyone else
   so that they do not have to think; they simply want to be one
   of the group or the crowd. Yet they also realise that this is a
   denial of their capabilities, and it is this denial that leads to
   despair. They may seek to suppress any awareness of their
   human capacities and therefore to hide from themselves the
   fact that they are in despair. In this case individuals may be in

---

* Søren Kierkegaard, *The Sickness unto Death*, pp. 49, 50.

despair without realising it.

2. Individuals can fall into despair as a result of wanting to assert themselves and to be themselves on their own terms. This happens when the ego is at the centre of their lives and they live for themselves alone. In this case, their ego constructs a self purely based on their own self-interest. Living for self has become such a total focus of their life that they become manacled in despair to the self they have constructed. They have decided to centre their lives on self but, deep down, they recognise that this cannot provide fulfilment and therefore they are in despair, even if they attempt to hide this from themselves.

3. Individuals can fall into despair as a result of conforming to society or to some institutional, religious or political system and to seek to find meaning in this way – but the meaning often comes to be seen as a construct which cannot withstand the problems and disasters which life throws up. What appears so secure when times are good can easily dissolve when faced with a real crisis or even with serious illness or death. Most of the time people in this state will appear content and secure and awareness of despair will only surface at occasional moments when the apparent security is challenged and undermined.

All of these can represent ways in which individuals avoid confronting themselves and avoid facing up to their true potential as human beings. They are ways of clinging on to a low level understanding of what it is to be human and refusing to attempt to fulfil human potential and they can all lead to despair even if this feeling is repressed. One of the few ways to address this is for them to be prepared to be still and silent, to begin an inward journey and to come to 'know themselves', but this will be hard and painful and most prefer to avoid taking this route.

Happiness

Most people wish to be happy, and it seems a reasonable thing to wish. People constantly wish this for others - they say 'Happy

Birthday', 'Happy New Year', 'Happy Christmas', 'Have a happy holiday' or 'Have a happy day'. The surprising thing is that few people ever ask what 'being happy' means or challenge the assumptions on which it is based. Most people want a happy marriage, a happy family life or a happy retirement. Happiness seems to be the thing that is desired more than anything else. The philosophic theory, utilitarianism, claims that what is good is represented by that which generates the most happiness. Happiness is sought by young people as an aim in life, it is hoped for by newly weds, and it is looked forward to by those anticipating retirement. It is, then, strange that none of the great world religious leaders have ever promised their followers happiness, in fact quite the reverse. Jesus told his followers that they would be persecuted, scourged, imprisoned and put to death – and this was the path that they were meant to choose. Clearly he was working with a rather different view of happiness from Father Christmas, the tooth fairy, Easter bunnies or the consumers of McDonald's 'happy meals'. If there is a single human nature and if the task of life is to fulfil this nature, then this will not be done by seeking to be happy. Seeking happiness as the prime aim in life will just prevent individuals from facing up to the challenge of becoming fully human.

Happiness is often the state of those in despair who have striven successfully to hide from themselves that they are in despair. It is the opposite of the state of those in anguish or despair – indeed, happiness is the very reverse of these states. The films *American Beauty* and *Happiness* starkly reveal the misery concealed beneath the happy exterior of much of American society. The point of both films is to make clear that this concealment is only partial. They attempt to reveal the efforts people make to maintain mechanisms in place which prevent them recognising their despair. The idea that people can find happiness by buying things or making lifestyle choices, or even by falling in love, entering a new relationship or getting what they want, is based on a fiction.

The Buddha recognised this. Desire, he considered, lay at the heart of the problem of being human and, until individuals stopped desiring those things which could not bring satisfaction, they could not begin the journey on the path to enlightenment.

The Buddha wanted his followers to extinguish not desire itself but the wrong sort of desire – desire that conceals reality, that masks the real nature of the human condition. The Buddha wanted people to rid themselves of false desires or bad faith as these amount to constructing their selves on sand.

The question can be expressed by asking 'What do you really desire?' or, to put it another way, 'What do you really love?' The following answers may be given:

- 'To be happy'. This is a common answer, and what it really means is that people desire whatever will bring them short-term pleasure. They will be motivated to action by passing moods and inclinations and have not reflected deeply on what they want or why they are alive.
- 'To please myself, to be independent'. This is an honest answer which not many may give (which does not mean it may not be quite commonly true – cf. chapter eight). These people are really in love with themselves; they have placed self at the centre of their lives. Their only criterion is what they want: they have no regard for others or for any other goal other than what will suit them.
- 'To live a good life'. For rare individuals who seek to lead an ethical life (see chapter nine), then the centre of their lives is the ethical choices they have made, on which and through which they construct their identity. A good example is a marriage, in which a couple enters into a freely chosen and irrevocable commitment to stay together and constructs their identity within the framework they have chosen.

The Buddha taught that individuals needed to see through the illusion of false desire for things that will make them happy and instead to seek enlightenment. They needed to come to recognise that none of the above would bring fulfilment. According to the Buddha, the only way to avoid suffering (and he was really talking of the suffering that comes from different levels of despair) is to avoid attachment to worldly things. Worldly pleasures, sensual enjoyment, success, praise, possessions, etc., all need to be subordinated to the goal of enlightenment since it is through centring one's life on these things that suffering arises. Individuals should aim to realise their true state and begin to address it. All humans are immersed in *samsara* which refers to the human state of wandering through life in ignorance and in illusion. In this respect, the Buddha's teachings are closely related to the central teaching of the Hebrew Scriptures.

Idol worship

The single sin which the Hebrew Scriptures condemn more than any other is fornication – but this has nothing to do with sex. Instead, it amounts to idolatry. The Hebrew Scriptures raise no problem with the fact that King Solomon had many wives – many of them foreign – but they do condemn him for fornicating after other gods, in other words for worshipping other gods, which was idolatry. The first and second of the Ten Commandments prohibit idolatry. Today the gods people worship are not made of wood, stone or bronze, instead they are more potent gods – the gods of self-interest, happiness and bad faith. These gods manifest themselves in many different forms. Many worship at the altars of the god of sport, the god of money, the god of pride, the god of lifestyle, the god of reputation, the god of sex. Most people have a whole plethora of gods which they worship as they pass through life. Human beings have not changed much since ancient times when people worshipped the gods of the rivers, trees and mountains. Today almost everyone has their own gods to whom they offer temporary obeisance before moving on to the next one. The gods vary depending on the culture, and in liberal democracies people tend to respect each other's gods – they may even sometimes worship at shrines which they normally ignore. Some may have no sporting interest until their national team is involved in a major clash and does very well. Then they quickly also participate in the rituals demanded before moving on. Most people, of course, do not think that they have any gods at all, just as the people of Israel did not at first understand why they were being criticised by the prophets for their idolatry.

The Hebrew and Christian Scriptures both expressly state that men and women shall not love, obey, bow down to or worship *any* other gods than the true God under any circumstance – in other words they prohibit idolatry. Islam takes this sin more seriously than any other religion and, within Islam, it is condemned more strongly than anything else. The Qu'ran records how the first Muslim, Abraham, came to realise there was only one god. He tried to persuade his father and his family that they should abandon their worship of many gods, but none of them listened to him. Abraham* was the first monotheist, the first uncompromising worshipper of a single God. Finding himself ignored in his own town and by his own family, he broke into the temple at night and, according to the Hadith, destroyed with an axe all the idols there – except for the largest one. When the destruction was discovered the next morning Abraham was suspected, but he replied to the charges levelled against him that the biggest idol must have destroyed the others. This was a clever answer as each idol was considered to be a god. His opponents could hardly, therefore, deny the power of the biggest god to act. Nevertheless they refused to believe him and threw him into the fire. God intervened to save him, saying, 'Oh fire, be coolness and safety to Abraham', and it was after this that Abraham left Ur and began his wanderings. Similarly, the prophet Muhammad destroyed all the idols in the temple at Mecca demanding that only one god should be acknowledged.

The destruction of idols was and is central to Judaism and Islam. Having rejected idols, it was a fairly simple matter for both these religions to substitute worship of a single God. The situation today is more complex. In a world dominated by postmodernism there is a general denial of any ultimate truth and getting rid of idols then appears to leave a vacuum. Postmodernism emphasises the pointlessness not just of idols but of any search for meaning. This, surprisingly, does have one advantage in that it can help people to recognise life as meaningless and thereby to force people closer to despair. What it fails

---

* The Qu'ran is very clear that it is Abraham and not Muhammad who was the first Muslim as it was Abraham who was the first to submit to God and to be obedient to God.

to do is to equip them with any way forward. The result will often be taking refuge in work, activity, alcohol or even drugs as ways of avoiding facing despair. It is precisely this situation that needs to be tackled.

Religion can be seen in two ways:

1. It can be a crutch to give comfort to the troubled soul – in this case, it is another distraction, another way of avoiding confronting the self.

2. It can provide a way for people to come to see the truth about the human condition, enabling them to fulfil their potential, and nourishing, feeding, watering and strengthening their self. The self can then find freedom from fear, it can acquire the power of discernment and also find the strength of will to make choices to live a good life which goes beyond standard ethical categories. This is the response of the truly religious in spirit.

When it is viewed in the second of these two ways, religion can provide a reply to postmodernism, but since it is usually understood in the first way it is seen as irrelevant to contemporary life. Religion, in the second sense, can call individuals to the possibilities of which they are capable, calling them to fulfil their potential and to ignore the relative gods which are so attractive and persuasive but which provide no meaning and no hope.

As was seen in chapter three, Aristotle considered that a frog that was asleep was not fulfilling all the potential of a frog. Many potentialities lay dormant, awaiting the frog's awakening to a life of eating bugs, communicating with other frogs, mating and doing all the things that adult frogs do. Perhaps, of course, human beings are just animals and they equally fulfil their potential simply by eating, communicating with others, breeding, caring for their young – effectively, therefore, being no different than frogs, apart from the fact that they are more complex.

It is the argument of this book that many human beings are, like the sleeping frog, asleep to their true potentialities and despair occurs because these potentialities are not realised.

Any new approach to ethics must address the despair and lack of meaning that is common to human beings, both its psychological origins as well as charting a way forward which is firmly grounded in what it is to be human. The great strength of such an approach is that it eliminates so many of the national, racial, gender, sexual, age or other differences that individuals seek to erect to emphasise their differences. If every person is equally human and if everyone has the potential to become fully human, then the way is open for a morality that applies to all people. This is the great advantage of the Natural Law approach to ethics as it does not depend on revelation or inspiration by a particular group – it depends on clear and sound philosophical thinking to work out what it is to be human. *In the remaining chapters it will be argued that just as a child has the potential to become an adult, so an adult has the ability to realise his or her potential and to become a full human being. In the case of many people, however, this potential remains dormant and is not realised.*

The exercise of potential involves humans being free to make choices – to decide for themselves whether they will be content with simply being a fully grown human animal or whether they will choose to use their freedom to become something great by realising the common potential that all human beings share. However, many deny that human beings are free and this is the next issue that needs to be considered.

Necessity and possibility

The human psyche was studied more in the twentieth century than ever before. It is extremely complex and can be likened to a house with a myriad rooms. Understanding it verges on the impossible. No wonder it is so hard for us to understand ourselves! Some of the rooms are clean and well swept, open to visitors and people feel at ease there. Other rooms are more shadowy, less welcoming: we do not like to enter these rooms in our own psyche and we allow only close friends access. Others are even murkier and these are scarcely ever visited. Still others, however, lurk dark and airless, unopened and unexamined.*

---

* I am not sure of the source of this image but I am aware that it is not original to me!

However, it is these unexplored rooms that largely determine who we are, that guide our thoughts and motivate our actions. It is these rooms that are in the driving seat, whilst the drunken peasant that most of us represent lies asleep in the cart being driven we know not where.

The mysterious depths of the human psyche fuel and contribute to the human sense of anguish and despair. These forces seem to bind individuals in an iron grip destroying any potential, any ability to change or to become other than what we are. It is easy to see ourselves as necessitated beings, ruled by forces beyond our control. In the Middle Ages these forces were expressed in terms of demons and devils, which seemed to provide plausible explanations for human actions – indeed, some were tempted to abdicate any sense of personal responsibility by saying 'the devil made me do it'. Even St Paul said, 'The good that I would do, I do not, the evil that I would not do, that I do.'* St Paul, great saint that he was, recognised the forces acting on him. Today genetics or psychological conditioning provide an alternative vehicle to explain these forces and these seem far more plausible than the devil – thus people can absolve themselves from responsibility (and hence from the demands of freedom) by seeing themselves as genetically determined.

For human beings seeing themselves as determined by factors beyond their control leads to despair. It means that they are puppets in the service of the determining factors that control them. People who are determined have no hope and no ability to change their condition since they are locked in by forces that are beyond their control. Any freedom they may experience is felt to be an illusion since the idea that they can do what they want or wish, is nothing more than a feeling. If what individuals want or wish is wholly determined, then any apparent freedom they think they have is illusory, and it is easy to see why they readily despair at the bleak condition in which they find themselves.

If human beings are really determined, then they are no more than puppets. Any idea of ethics disappears, and Mother Teresa and Hitler are morally equivalent since they were both wholly

---

* Romans 7:19.

determined. There are many ways to argue determinism. These include:

1. psychological determinism – which maintains that nature and nurture, from a very early age, determine who a person is. He or she is incapable of acting against the determination laid down in infancy;
2. genetic determinism – which sees character traits and behaviour from criminality to drunkenness to sexual behaviour as being genetically determined and therefore beyond individual control;
3. sociological determinism – which sees society exercising such power over individuals that they are determined by the community in which they live;
4. divine determinism – which sees God as determining everything individuals do. This amounts, of course, to predestination and is a particular problem for Calvinistic Christianity as well as for Islam where everything is held to happen by the will of God.

All these are possible positions but if any one of them is true, then there is no possibility of human beings, by their own efforts, altering what they are pre-determined to do. It is precisely the individual's awareness of freedom that undermines the determinist position and gives rise to anxiety, anguish and despair. If human beings were simply programmed robots, this despair would not arise – and from that point of view anguish and despair can be forms of hope as they can be a recognition of freedom.

- It is freedom that leads individuals out of conformity and lack of reflection about who they are.
- It is freedom that challenges the comfort zone of convention often provided by ethical rules.
- It is freedom that challenges the ego when it wishes to enslave human beings to their own petty desires.
- It is freedom that, in the final analysis, may lead individuals to see through even their own ethical commitments and begin to question them.

It is precisely this freedom that opens the door to a spiritual understanding of what it is to be human and that opens the possibility of taking individuals beyond the animal stage to a higher level of fulfilment. This is crucial if individuals are to realise their potential and yet it is constantly ignored.

The more successful people are in suppressing their freedom, the closer they are to a form of living death – to inhabiting the comfort zone of convention. However, people can never really die in this way as freedom constantly wells up to challenge them. Freedom has, therefore, to be constantly suppressed by the ego to avoid the anguish and despair that it brings.

The alternative to necessity is possibility. Necessity sees human beings as determined, locked into genetic and socially conditioned patterns from which they cannot escape. Possibility rejects this view and affirms the possibility of human freedom, the openness to those suppressed well springs that can be released to allow individuals to choose what they wish to become.

Freedom as an achievement

Freedom, on this view, is not something that human beings either have or do not have. This has been the mistake made by so many philosophers who have tried to wrestle with the question of whether or not humans are free. It is more plausible to see human beings as being in the grip of necessity but with the possibility of freedom ever open, ever waiting to be realised if they have the courage and, perhaps, the strength to make use of it.

Human beings are not all free, most of them are in chains. Plato recognised this in his myth in which he saw people bound in a cave, locked into shadows. The Buddha recognised this and so did St Paul. The people in the film *The Matrix* were not free: they were bound into a world of illusion and, even when they were made free (as Cypher was in the film), some wished only to return to their original state of bondage. The possibility of freedom is always open but the road to achieve it is hard and difficult.

The possibility of freedom is the central uniting insight of major religious and philosophic traditions.

- The Buddhist tradition regards this world as a world of illusion. The first task, the Buddha maintained, is to see the illusion for what it is and then to seek right knowledge of the situation human beings face. The Buddha considered the path to this knowledge to be exceptionally difficult. It involves individuals taking control of their minds which they normally allow to control them, flitting about from one concern to the next.
- Plato considered that human beings have to be set free from the chains that imprison them in the cave of ignorance. They could do this, he maintained, by learning, through philosophy, to control the mind. He expressed this by saying that the task of each individual in life is to preserve their soul which he considered to be constantly corrupted and undermined by the body within which it is imprisoned.
- Aristotle considered that part of being human is having the potential to realise our true nature. However, this nature often languished unfulfilled and individuals have to use their intellect in order to realise their true potential.
- Jesus said that becoming one of his followers would bring freedom because following him necessitated cutting themselves loose from the normal chains of life and living life in a radically different way free from the prison of self or from the chains of convention and culture.
- The Sufi mystics considered that it was only by individuals freeing themselves from the conventions of everyday existence and seeking to centre their life on God that freedom could be achieved. They maintained that this wisdom, found in contemplation and stillness, exceeded the knowledge found in philosophy in the same way that the understanding of an adult exceeded that of a child.
- Branches of Hinduism advocate the seeking of enlightenment and wisdom after the normal duty of family life has been completed and this means renouncing normal life in order to live a much simpler and more spiritual form of existence.
- Immanuel Kant did not think that human freedom could be

proved, but considered that freedom was a necessary postulate of any morality. If human beings are bound by the chains of necessity then morality does not exist as all human actions, whether for good or ill, are wholly determined.

Some, of course, deny that there is any possibility of human beings being released from the chains of necessity. When individuals see themselves as being locked into a hopeless position from which they cannot escape, they despair. They see their condition as without hope as it is without possibility. They see themselves as necessitated by forces beyond their control. The lack of hope is precisely a denial of possibility and an affirmation of necessity – once hope is lost, then all alternatives are closed down except those which lead to despair. It is precisely this apparent lack of hope which lies beneath the human condition as it is perceived by most people. Once individuals allow themselves the space to recognise it, they will see it is an almost universal human condition. Normally individuals will do everything possible to avoid giving themselves this space, precisely because to do so means opening the possibility that despair will emerge. They thus avoid the reality of the despair by keeping themselves so busy that they do not even see it. Instead, they convince themselves that they are 'happy' or content, that there is nothing else that they want and they reject any attempt to think more deeply about who they are. Doing this, individuals prevent themselves making any progress at all on the path to becoming more fully human, to realising more fully the potential of which they are capable (and what this means still needs to be spelt out).

Despair thus lies at the gateway to hope. It is like a great fire-breathing dragon which individuals will do everything to avoid because they fear it will lead to their destruction. Real despair is an appalling condition. Depression is a pale reflection of despair. Indeed, depression and despair may not be related. Clinical depression is a disease that can be diagnosed and treated. Despair falls into a different category entirely. It saps the very being of individuals, challenges who a person is and renders all relationships, all activities and all aspiration empty and futile. It can easily lead to suicide as life seems devoid of any meaning or any hope – according to a World Health Organisation report over 816,000 people attempted suicide in the latest year for which statistics are available. Sometimes no success, however great, can provide meaning; no affirmation can undermine the reality of the despair. All that most people can attempt is to seek oblivion to its reality by throwing themselves into activity. This is precisely why stillness and silence are seen as such a threat: once a person is silent then the dragon of despair rears its head once more and roars ever more fiercely, forcing them to throw themselves back into activity and complacency.

Yet it is precisely through the doorway guarded by the dark dragon of despair that hope may lie. Hope depends on accepting the possibility that freedom brings; hope is the antidote to despair; hope is grounded in the ability to change ourselves and to find, against all hope, that a person has become what he or she is capable of becoming.

- It is this further stage represented by the Natural Law tradition which most modern materialist writers neglect or dismiss.
- It is this further stage that concentration on genetics and what it is to be a physical human being completely ignores.
- It is this further stage which takes seriously the potential of human beings to move beyond their biological adulthood and to become fully mature human beings.

This requires an individual to fulfil their psychological and spiritual potential. This is a hard and dangerous journey, past the dragon of despair and it involves a number of stages.

The Implications for Ethics

There is extraordinary unity among all the world religions and even amongst atheist philosophers such as Sartre. There is the recognition that human fulfilment demands that individuals rid themselves of false gods, stripping away all those things that disguise reality and hide the truth about life's apparent meaninglessness. If individuals fail to do this, then they will not have any possibility of fulfilling their human nature. Despair will constantly lurk beneath their lives, ready to reach out and engulf them, to overwhelm and drown them in a tide of meaninglessness and emptiness. The antidote to the feeling of being determined, of being locked in to a cycle of meaninglessness, is found in the recognition that other possibilities are open to them and it is this that despair refuses to recognise.

It is precisely this psychological truth, to which all major religions testify, which needs to be taken into account in any contemporary understanding of ethics. The psychological truth that the lives of many people rest in despair is ignored in almost all contemporary and classical discussions of ethics, yet it is fundamental. If ethics is grounded, as Aristotle and the European tradition have affirmed, in what it is to be human, then the psychological state of human beings is part of the ethical equation. This state is one of constant hunger and thirst and longing for meaning. If this thirst is not satisfied, then anguish and despair occur. Only a response which takes the spiritual possibility of human beings seriously can provide a permanent release.

If individuals begin to strip away their desire for the false gods they have constructed, then despair will arise from the chasm of emptiness. This is terrifying for the ego – to be alone, with its soul empty of those distractions which mollify and lull the self into a false sense of security. Truth, however frightening, grounds the individual and allows the possibility of selfhood to emerge through the development of the spiritual side of human life.

To be fully human means to recognise the spiritual aspect of human life as well as the physical. This is why concentration on genetics can be so very dangerous because it leads us to focusing only on one part of what it is to be human – and probably the least important part. The spiritual side, towards which all the great religions point, is wholly ignored. This insight, however, needs to be unpacked and developed.

11

Moving Beyond
the Dragon

Human beings are far more fragile and more vulnerable than most philosophers accept. John Cottingham and Alastair MacIntyre are two modern philosophers who have both acknowledged this. John Cottingham in a paper said the following:

It is curious how little these basic features of human existence [dependency, finitude and mortality] are acknowledged and reflected upon in the voluminous writings of moral philosophers. This is a point nicely brought out in Alastair MacIntyre's most recent book, aptly named *Dependent Rational Animals*:

'[There are facts] ... concerning our vulnerabilities and afflictions and those concerning the extent of our dependence on particular others so evidently of singular importance that it might seem that no account of the human condition whose authors hoped to achieve credibility could avoid giving them a central place. Yet the history of Western moral philosophy suggests otherwise. From Plato to Moore and since there are usually, with some rare exceptions, only passing reference to human vulnerability and affliction and to the connections between them and our dependence on others ... Moral agents are presented as though they were continuously rational, healthy and untroubled ...'

... this is a kind of arrogance about the powers of human reason: we, the philosophers, take ourselves to have the wisdom to lay down a recipe for the good life, and we, the scientists, claim to have the theoretical knowledge and technical know-how to achieved the desired result.*

The arrogance of both philosophers and scientists in seeking to claim that they can solve the problems facing human beings is staggering – yet it goes almost unchallenged. The danger of defining human beings simply in physical terms is that a whole dimension of what it is to be human is missed out – this includes not only human vulnerability, morality and dependency but also a broader and more positive dimension. The religious perspective on life has always stood for the claim that there is a transcendent dimension to human existence. The first part of this book considered the physical dimension to being fully human. However, the religious perspective claims that spiritual development is even more important. It is easy to regard human beings as being simply animals, in the grip of necessity, determined by their genetics and their human nature. It is easy to assume that human destiny is under human control and, given time, scientists will sort out the problems – however, this is not the case. Human beings are mortal. Despair stalks their lives and, unless this is first acknowledged, there is no way forward. Talk of the spiritual side of human nature affirms the importance of a transcendental dimension, driven by the possibility of freedom. No matter what people have done or what lives they have led, they can use freedom to begin afresh and start again on the task of fulfilling their potential.

It is as if human beings have a task in life which is to create an incredible sculpture, but the sculpture that they are called upon to create is themselves. This is why the question 'What sort of person shall I become?' is far more significant and profound than the question 'What shall I do?' The problem is that it is a hard question to answer as there is no single picture of what all human beings should be. It is one thing to say that all human beings share a common nature grounded in what it is to be human but this certainly does not mean that all human beings

---

* Given to the Philosophy Society at Heythrop College, University of London, on 23 September 2002.

are the same. Hair, skin colour, height, intelligence and many other factors cause immense variations between individuals, yet in spite of this every individual is a human being.

What, then, might lie beyond the dragon of despair that might provide a path forward so that individual and very different human beings can all seek to realise their full potential? This is the most important and most difficult question that ethics, psychology, theology and philosophy have to answer and their success in doing so has been very limited indeed. Some will, of course, deny that there is any question to address since all that being human means is to live a busy and active life centred either on self, ethics or, probably, having no centre at all and reacting to events as they occur. The religious perspective claims that there is something more.

Crucially the religious perspective holds that beyond vulnerability and despair lies hope and that there is wisdom available to enable human beings to find this hope and gain insight into the nature of what it is to fulfil their potential. This insight may well not be achievable by reason alone: something more may be required which rationality alone may be incapable of finding.

Wisdom

Immanuel Kant argued that there were three fundamental questions:
1. What can I know?
2. What should I do?
3. What can I hope for?

Kant was in many ways a philosopher's philosopher. He was suspicious of the emotions: for him, reason reigned supreme and the human task was to develop a 'good will' by acting wholly in accordance with reason. Yet Kant himself recognised that this analysis was not adequate and, although many philosophers do not like to admit it and although they often omit this side of his philosophy, he regarded faith as being of central importance and said that an action by God was needed, through the Christian incarnation, to release human beings from the self-imposed chains of necessity. Reason is vital but it does not have the final answer to the problem of human existence.

This limitation on the role of reason is something that philosophers have not always recognised. Philosophy is, after all, a rational activity. For Aristotle the faculty of understanding was the highest part of human beings, distinguishing them from the animals. Through the use of reason human beings could understand the essential nature of things – not just things as they appear, but what made everything what it was and what made it do what it did. This is a rational activity and is represented by the paradigm case of science. There is no doubt that Aristotle – and the long line of philosophers since – was right to emphasise the rational side of human beings in that it is through reason that human beings can work out how to live. However, one cannot analyse the fullness of what it is to be human solely in rational terms. At the least, there are in addition the emotional and relational sides of being human, and concentration on reason only can easily lead to these being overlooked. Many modern feminist philosophers have recognised this and have seen the emphasis on reason alone as accentuating a particular, male paradigm of what it is to be human with none of the need for relationship that is so vital to the feminine side of the human person.

Reason, therefore, may not be able to answer all the questions about human existence. Kant thought that reason was sufficient to decide on what individuals should do, but this takes no account of human emotions or the complexity of relationships to which individuals are committed. Still less can it provide a full account of what it is to be human and what humans can hope for through reason alone.

If human beings are locked into the cycle of self, then there is no answer to the last of Kant's questions about what can be hoped for – except possibly a life filled with isolated pleasures, an absence of pain and then death. The religious perspective claims there is something more. However, if humans are simply glorified animals, 'robot vehicles blindly programmed to preserve the selfish molecules known as genes',[*] then necessity

---

[*] Richard Dawkins in *The Selfish Gene* (Oxford, Oxford Paperbacks, 1989).

seems to rule and despair is a logical outcome. Once, however, it is accepted that past mistakes do not lock individuals into a downward spiral, once forgiveness for past mistakes is a possibility, then hope arises. It is like a very small, mute child hidden inside every person, whose very existence is suppressed.

Hope is the child of possibility and is often born of despair. However, it is only when a person can feel forgiven, when they can put the guilt of the past behind them that the issue of what can be hoped for surfaces, not just as an intellectual question but as a practical one. They can then ask: 'Is there any hope beyond the dragon?', 'Has life any meaning and how can this provide guidance as to how life should be lived?', 'Is there a way forward?'

In the days of Socrates, Plato and Aristotle philosophy was concerned with the search for wisdom and the search for an understanding of how each individual should live. Today, in a postmodern world, 'wisdom' is an unusual word to find in a philosophy book, but this was not always the case. The ancient Greek philosophers were occupied with the search for wisdom and this search precisely represented the possibility individuals have, as human beings, to be more than can be contained in any physical description. It is the omission of this possibility that is such a damaging part of the state of human beings today.

The motto of the Greek God Apollo, 'Know yourself' is, perhaps, the hardest task any human being can face. Wisdom and knowledge of ourselves do not come from learned philosophic journals. The professional philosophers that inhabit university departments may be cleverer than others but few of them are wiser. Wisdom requires the integration of a whole range of disciplines and does not come from intellectual study alone. It is the child of experience, adversity and failure. It demands integration of many elements which make up the life of a fulfilled human being.

Perspicuity

Wittgenstein was probably the most important and significant philosopher of the twentieth century, although the precise nature of his contribution is much disputed. Possibly the key word in the whole of Wittgenstein's philosophy was 'perspicuity'[*] (another similar word used by the Catholic philosopher Bernard Lonergan was 'insight'). Wittgenstein's whole life was deeply committed to seeking to understand the nature of human beings, human language and how individuals should act. Wittgenstein was in many ways a deeply religious man, but not in a conventional sense. He was deeply serious about himself, about what it was to be a self, and about how life should be lived, and he sought a perspicuous understanding of the nature of the human condition and how this should be lived out. His was not simply a philosophy of the lecture room but rather a philosophy that affected every aspect of his life – it was in this sense that he was so serious. He greatly admired the philosophic giants of the past as they shared a similar seriousness about life. They staked their lives on the search for wisdom and for truth, as did he.

Even the most banal of Wittgenstein commentators would not say that there is any ethical system that can be described as his. He wrestled throughout his life with profound ambiguity, seeking the right way to live, sometimes in solitude as when he spent a year in a small hut on the banks of a fjord in Norway – but always paying serious attention to how his life should be spent. Perspicuity recognises complexity and attempts to grapple with it. Perspicuity attempts to see beyond the superficial and the obvious to the depth of what lies beyond. Perspicuity resists 'doing violence' through simplistic interpretations of the human condition.

It is so easy to judge others, to impose one's own conceptions on the lives of others. Some so-called religious people are experts at this, branding as 'sinners' those who do not conform to their own simplistic rules. Perspicuity recognises human complexity and understands that judging other people is almost always done with inadequate understanding and information. Jesus condemned those who judged others and for good reason as judgement is always made with inadequate information. It fails

---

[*] This is well brought out by Felicity McCutcheon's important book *Religious Within the Limits of Language* (Aldershot, Ashgate, 1991).

to understand complexity and lacks perspicuity. Those who have wrestled with the complexity of life, who have lived serious lives seeking to wrestle with the difficulty of the human condition, know that simple judgements are almost always inaccurate and lack wisdom.

Seriousness in itself is part of the search for perspicuity but it is not the same as perspicuity. It comes from the recognition of the absolute demand made on each person to become a self, to fulfil his or her potential, to become what every human being is capable of being. However, insight is required to understand what this is and the radical consequences of being mistaken.

Perspicuity and wisdom are not things that merely happen to anyone. They are achievements, and many people who seek them for most of their lives may never attain them. Wisdom has the peculiar feature that the more it is sought, the further the person seeking may appear to be from the object of their search. Socrates felt that he knew nothing and, when the Delphi Oracle described him as the wisest man in Athens, he was so sure that this was an error that he set out to prove the Oracle wrong. In a similar way the great saints of the Christian tradition often acknowledged themselves as the greatest of sinners. This is not perversity, still less a glorying in contradiction, but rather a recognition that the more individuals understand themselves, the more they achieve wisdom and a perspicuous understanding of what it is to be human, the further they realise they are from the ideal.

Perspicuity enables human beings to probe the complexity of what it is to be human. Wisdom may be the child of the search, but understanding ourselves in itself will not bring wisdom. It will only be a beginning of the path. The achievement of wisdom demands something more, and there is a key ingredient which has to underlie any ethical system and any idea of what it is to be fully human. This ingredient is accountability.

Accountability

Central to the search for wisdom in the sense in which the word has been used by most of the great philosophers of the past and by all great religious thinkers is the idea of accountability. All human beings are accountable for their actions but they are even more accountable for the selves that they build. *It is in living a life that is radically accountable that selfhood emerges.* Different thinkers have expressed this in different terms but the underlying message is the same – it is in being accountable that selfhood emerges, and it is this understanding of accountability and the accompanying development of self that can provide hope beyond the dragon.

Four examples of the centrality of accountability in the search for wisdom will illustrate its importance:

1. Socrates and Plato held that every human being was accountable for the self and they expressed this in their talk of the soul. They believed that after death all human beings would be held accountable for the lives they had lived, and it is for this reason that they considered that it was better to suffer harm than to inflict it. Socrates' hearers could not understand him when he said this, but he considered it to be self-evident. If individuals suffer harm, then they can absorb the pain and it does not affect their inmost nature, but when they inflict harm they damage themselves most of all. All people have a duty in life to care for their soul and this means preventing their bodies taking over so that they come to act simply out of animal desire and inclination in ways that will damage the soul. All human beings are accountable for the self they construct and will have to render an account, so Plato and Socrates considered, when they go before the Judges after death.

2. The Buddha considered that all human beings are accountable to themselves for the lives they lead. The self they construct will determine what happens in their next life. However, to talk of people being accountable to themselves does not mean that they can live in whatever way they choose – the Buddha recognised the common nature of all humanity and saw the human task as being to pierce through the veil of illusion (*samsara*) with which everyone is surrounded in order to achieve a true understanding of how to live. Only when they correctly understand the nature of their current position can

they begin on the long hard path towards enlightenment. This is the very reverse of simply following individual selfish inclinations. Every person has the chance to free themselves from the prison of desire and to achieve enlightenment, but they are responsible and accountable for their own actions in doing this. They cannot escape the inevitable and inexorable effect that their adverse actions have on themselves when they fail to accept or take seriously the reality that every action has an effect on who a person is.

3. Central to the Hebrew, Christian and Islamic traditions is the importance of being accountable to God for every word and every action. There is no commandment more important than the one which commands love, obedience and loyalty to one God. There is no sin that is more grievous nor carries more serious consequences than idolatry. Judaism, Christianity and Islam are very clear that the task of every human being is to place God at the centre of the whole of their lives and, when they do this, they will achieve the highest good that is possible for human beings. This is not because of some simplistic idea of a heavenly reward handed out to those who do as they are told by the great power figure in the sky. It is a far more profound sense of an understanding that every human being is made for fellowship with God – this is the end, according to the monotheistic tradition, for which human beings are made, this is the purpose of their existence. Anything less than this is an impoverished vision of the human condition.

4. Vaclav Havel, poet, philosopher, playwright and President of the Czech Republic, stood against the power of the communist State which oppressed the people of Czechoslovakia. He was imprisoned for four years and throughout this period and subsequently he argued in his books, his letters, his poetry and his plays, the need for every individual to be radically accountable to something ultimate beyond the confines of their own psyche and community. For him, the chief problem of his country under communism lay in the willingness of citizens to conform, to judge their lives and their actions by the accepted standards of their society. If these standards were unjust, then there was no way of appealing beyond them and

standing in opposition to them. It is for this reason that he argued that accountability to something ultimate is so essential – only this can provide the possibility of standing against the values of an individual's own society.

When a nation, society, community or religious grouping holds there is no higher authority than its own ethics, institutional evil may occur. This is because there is no sense of responsibility to something ultimate beyond the ethics of the community. This lack of responsibility to something ultimate – which many call God – prevents any challenge to the evil perpetuated by communities and societies. It is only in being accountable to something ultimate and non-relative that notions such as Justice, Truth and Morality can be sustained in anything other than a relativistic, postmodern sense. It is the denial of such an ultimate that leads to the present human state of ethical impotence. However, problems also occur in the case of fundamentalists, who see themselves as accountable to an ultimate they often call God and, out of loyalty to this ultimate, seek to impose their view of truth on all others. Accountability, therefore, has to be understood in a way which can avoid the mistakes of fundamentalism, and this will be addressed in the final chapter.

Accountability is vital to any understanding of what it is to be human. But it is not simply any form of accountability. Earlier chapters outlined the impoverished view of what it is to be human that arises:

1. when human beings are accountable only to themselves (chapter eight), or
2. when human beings are accountable only to the community of which they form part (chapter nine).

Still more impoverished are lives lived without any form of accountability whatsoever. These are those with no centre to their lives (chapter seven) – to use a previous example, like the drunken man asleep in the cart pulled by horses which go wherever they will.

It may be, of course, that life has no meaning and that there is nothing to be accountable to, except ourselves or the truths which we construct. Nietzsche took this view and rejected not just God but any ultimate meaning or value. He saw the role of the individual, who had the potential to become the superman, as being to transcend all the normal categories of right or wrong by being responsible only to self. This is the position of post-modernism with its rejection of any ultimate claims to truth and with its radical relativity. This is one possibility represented by (1) above. However, the options for accountability given above do not represent the only possibilities.

There is another form of accountability which the above positions do not recognise and, indeed, which they ignore and reject. This is accountability to something ultimate which some call God, others 'the transcendent' whilst others use other names. The existence of this reality cannot be proved and this is a good reason, some hold, to claim that it does not exist. Many attempts to achieve a satisfactory proof have been made. Philosophers have produced countless different arguments to try to prove the existence of God, but none of them succeed.* All depend for their validity on assumptions which believers will accept and non-believers reject. No one was ever persuaded to the truth of any transcendent reality by rational argument. Reason is vitally important for science, business and to make sense of much of our world but it has never provided a final determinant for religion, ethics, aesthetics, love or any of those aspects of human life that go beyond the material.

The logical positivists were a group of philosophers who were particularly influential between the two great world wars of the twentieth century. They held that, for a statement to have any meaning, it either had to be a tautology or it had to be verified empirically (using reason and observation). No statement that could not be verified had any meaning. This meant that all statements about religion, aesthetics, love and the like were dismissed as meaningless. This theory was shown to be radically flawed by Wittgenstein but it does not need any great

---

* The arguments are set out in *The Puzzle of God* by Peter Vardy (London, HarperCollins, 1999).

philosopher to show the error. The statement that 'all statements that cannot be verified empirically are meaningless' is itself meaningless. Lack of empirical proof does not render a statement meaningless. For instance, if someone claims 'human beings survive death' then there is no way that this can be proved to be either true or false – but this does not mean that it is not either true or false that human beings do survive death.

The claim that there is a God or a transcendent realm may not be provable but this does not mean there is not a truth at stake. Scientists today recognise that claims to truth do not depend on empirical evidence. Those working at the frontiers of science (for instance, in quantum physics) engage in speculations which to an outsider appear counter-intuitive and ridiculous, but nevertheless they are seeking a truthful understanding which conventional ways of measurement may be inadequate to grasp.[*]

Many people today are closet verificationists – in other words they assume (often without having analysed the assumption) that

---

[*] 'There are no analogies that we can carry over from our everyday experience into the world of the quantum, and the behavior of the quantum world is not like anything familiar. Nobody knows how the quantum world behaves the way it does, all we know is that it does behave the way it does', (John Gribben, *In Search of Schrodinger's Cat*, London, Corgi, 1985, p. 165). Imagine a box in which there is a live cat and a radioactive source. When an atomic nucleus from the radioactive source disintegrates, it releases an alpha particle which triggers the hammer and breaks poison. Quantum theory cannot predict the behaviour of any particle. If there is a 50 per cent chance of a particle being released, there is no way of telling whether the cat is alive or dead after a minute. However, quantum theory goes much further than this and says that there is no state of affairs until it is measured. So the alpha particle is neither released nor not released and the cat is neither alive or dead *until the box is opened*. Before this it is not just the case that we do not know whether the cat is alive or dead – the cat is both alive and dead! Schrodinger thought this was absurd and would disprove the quantum theory – but this is exactly what the theory says happens. It goes completely against 'common sense'. Einstein said that common sense was the series of prejudices a person accumulates by the time they are eighteen and great scientific advances are never made by those whose lives are constricted by the bounds of 'common sense'.

whatever is not provable by scientific methods is meaningless. However, this, when examined, proves to be a false assumption which will not bear the weight placed on it. Truth does not depend on evidence but on the state of affairs that is claimed to be true.

If there is a God or a transcendent 'Other', then lack of empirical proof does not mean that God does not exist. However, if there is a God or transcendent 'Other', then accountability for how human beings live does not just depend on accountability to community or to self. The possibility of being directly accountable to God or the transcendent then arises. Of course, this may be ignored, but the possibility is open. This possibility, of course, depends on whether there is a God or a transcendent reality and on the assumption that humans are more than just material beings, more than simply highly developed animals. If humans are content to see themselves as just glorified animals, then human potential is fulfilled simply by growing to be adult humans and doing the things that adult animals do – communicating, eating, forming relationships, reproducing and dying. This is Richard Dawkins' position. Dawkins claims that human beings are simply a biological accident. Life has no meaning and no purpose and human beings are simply the machines created by their genes to replicate and pass on these genes. Postmodernism fits well with this claim but this is precisely the claim that the great Greek philosophers, in particular Socrates, Plato and Aristotle, denied. Similarly the Christian tradition, that Aristotle so strongly influenced, and all the other major world religions reject Dawkins' analysis. They all affirm that there is more to being human than any material analysis can define.

One of the most striking features of the way certain strands of postmodernism have developed is that whilst God is rejected, nevertheless a commitment to an absolute idea of justice and a refusal to 'do violence' to others by imposing one's own categories or ideas have emerged as being of central importance.* However, few of the philosophers who talk in such

---

* Levinas is a good example of this – he affirms the absolute importance of justice but does not provide or attempt any rational justification for this claim.

terms address the issue of what underpins the demand of justice – and a transcendent Absolute has traditionally been regarded as the only feasible answer.

Stillness

Wisdom can only be sought and individuals can only come to know themselves if they are willing to provide themselves with the space to quieten the rush of activity in their lives and the even greater rush of mental activity in their heads. This entails a commitment to take time out from busyness, yet this is something most people are trained from an early age not to do. They are educated into seeing success and achievement solely in terms of outcomes and tasks accomplished, and the task of working on themselves to develop their self is considered of no importance and no account.

For the Buddhist, the path to freedom lies through stillness and meditation as it is only when individuals control their minds that they can seek to pierce through the veil of illusion and come to a full understanding of reality. In the Christian tradition, wisdom is seen as coming through prayer. Both approaches involve individuals being willing to be still, to stop their busyness and to ask fundamental questions which philosophers generally no longer ask.

To be willing to seek the wisdom that can come from stillness and silence and a lack of activity is generally a feature which comes with age. However, this is not necessarily the case. The young child delights in play, in being still, in lying on his or her back and looking at the clouds or even simply in day-dreaming. Soon, however, parents, teachers, television, the media and various peer groups all combine to reinforce the lesson that the only success worth having is outcome generated. Achievement in class, at home, on the PlayStation or the Nintendo become the name of the game. Sometimes such success is so obviously empty that one would have thought that anyone would have seen through it, but so strong is the culture of the times that the myth of activity is accepted without question.

Most people will acknowledge that they know many well-meaning, decent, individuals but few who have confronted the dragon of despair, few with any sense of inner peace, few with wisdom, few with any hope, few in whom they could recognise a quality that made them say, 'I wish I had that'. Nevertheless, a few such individuals do exist and their gentleness, their depth, their compassion, the sparkle in their eyes, their joy in life, combined with their profound identification with the world's sorrow and sadness are beacons of hope and possibility. In many, although not all, such cases the individuals are likely to be 'religious' people even if not all of them would identify with any conventional religion. They show what human nature can achieve at its best if the dark dragon is confronted and an attempt be made to seek to pierce through its guard to the sunnier pastures that lie beyond.

The Implications for Ethics

Part One of this book argued that enabling human beings to rectify defects and to enhance physical characteristics were both in accordance with the idea of becoming fully human. However, Part Two of the book has maintained that a full analysis of human nature extends far beyond this. If humans are to come to spiritual and psychological wholeness – and only by doing this can they move beyond the dragon of despair – then account-ability to something ultimate is vital. If Richard Dawkins is right, and life is meaningless and human beings are simply animals who have evolved by accident, then the dragon wins. There is no way beyond it. Human beings are locked into a cycle of meaningless and, whilst they can tell themselves stories that will convince themselves that life has some meaning, they are remorselessly driven back to the reality that it has not.

If, however, an Absolute (which some call God) exists, then everything changes. There is a way forward and it rests on the possibility of living the whole of one's life *coram deo* as Luther put it – before God.

At this point the key assumptions of this book need to be identified and clarified:

1. All human beings share a common human nature which can

be defined, as Aristotle suggested, in terms of human potentialities (chapters three and four).

2. This human nature can partly be defined in physical terms but it is more than this – there is a spiritual and psychological dimension that also needs to be fulfilled (chapter seven).

3. Failure to recognise this will lead to despair even though human beings do everything they can to conceal this despair from themselves (chapters eight to ten).

4. Human beings have a freedom which cannot be suppressed. Past failures can always be put in the past and a new start made (chapter ten).

5. If the existence of God or a transcendent other is accepted, then a life of radical accountability to this reality can provide hope and a way forward as well as an approach to ethics that is as relevant today as it has been for thousands of years (chapter eleven).

All these assumptions can be challenged – there is no way that they can be shown to be true using empirical science but that does not mean that they are false. It is precisely here that the problem arises. If human beings are more than rational animals, then the path to wisdom, perspicuity and insight into the human condition is not going to be achieved by reason alone.

Some things cannot be proved, they have to be seen.

Some things cannot be taught in the lecture room.

Some things cannot be learned from books.

This, however, does not mean that they are not real or true.

If perspicuity, insight and wisdom came from learning, then the most intelligent people would be the wisest – and they clearly are not. Plato thought that those who acted wrongly did so based on ignorance and that if people knew what was right they would do it, but in this he was mistaken. Knowledge does not lead to a higher ethical stance, to more fulfilled or more developed human beings. Knowledge alone is not enough. Human beings are incredibly complex and coming to wholeness means integrating the physical, emotional and psychological sides of our common humanity. Those people who are generally recognised for their wisdom, their depth and the fullness of their humanity are precisely those who have achieved this integration but they did not do so by having more intelligence or learning than others.

The truth about the human condition needs to be communicated indirectly, in ways that are not straightforward and without any guarantee that the communication will be successful. People need to be 'shown' what human beings are capable of becoming and only then, and not necessarily then, may they be willing to take in hand the change that is necessary so that they become a self – anchored not on personal whim, nor on community but on something ultimate which will endure and stand fast amidst all the changes of life and the world. Someone who is anchored in this way, who lives their life accountable to something ultimate, is invulnerable as their life does not depend on the contingencies of how things go. Even in death when job, possessions and even family fade into insignificance, this sense of accountability to something ultimate remains. The 'outcome' is no longer the determinant factor as what is important is the maintenance of fidelity to a commitment to the transcendent 'other' which grounds the self and provides a non-relative centre.

Such individuals can challenge institutional evil – the evils perpetrated by families, communities, nations, economic interests and religious groups – as they have a place to stand independent of them and a place from which the values of such institutions can be judged and questioned.

It is here that problems arise as the path to perspicuity, wisdom and insight is a path that every person has to travel alone. It is a path that leads through failure and despair, through inadequacy, and at times a sense of meaningless to something more. It is a path where success is not guaranteed and whose existence many would deny. However, in a postmodern world where the very idea of truth has become a dirty word, it is the only path that leads back to an understanding of human nature which takes seriously the modern ethical dilemmas faced by human beings whilst recognising the centrality of a psychological and spiritual perspective on human existence.

12

Living an
Accountable Life

Five themes have shaped this book:
1. the claim that the world has entered a time where meaning-lessness is endemic and where claims to absolute truth in morality and religion are, at the least, under threat or have been abandoned;
2. the argument that all human beings share a common human nature which can accommodate differences of colour, appearance, height, fingerprints, etc., and yet can still provide an understanding of ethics which is not relative to community, culture or institution;
3. the argument that it is right in principle to work towards helping people to overcome and correct illness and physical defects. The ethical use of the best medical science is the morally correct thing to do whether or not this involves genetic engineering provided that the rights of each person are respected and the possible unknown risks are first fully weighed and assessed;
4. the argument that human beings cannot be defined simply in physical terms and that what it is to be human transcends any mere physical or genetic description: it is to do with a spiritual side of human beings which, whilst difficult to define, is nevertheless common to all. This, it has been argued, is closely tied to the search for wisdom and a perspicuous under-standing of what it is to be human. This cannot be achieved by reason alone and yet it provides the only path for overcoming the dragon of despair and finding meaning and hope;

5. the argument that an accountable life, where accountability is not to self, nor to the ethical standards of the community in which a person lives, nor to the institutions to which he or she belongs but to a transcendent Other, which may or may not be called God, opens up the conceptual space for a way of living which is not relative to a particular society or to a particular interpretation of reality. This way of living can be committed to justice and goodness as objective standards grounded in a common human nature. It will also reject any actions which harm or diminish others as it will be committed to recognising the fundamental equality of all human beings and to helping other individuals to realise their full potential.

This last claim needs unpacking because not everyone will acknowledge such a transcendent Absolute and also because what it means to live an accountable life, even if such an Absolute exists, is not immediately clear.

All world religions hold to the idea of a transcendent reality which lies beyond the material world, except Buddhism. In Buddhism there is no idea of God or of a transcendent 'Other'. Nevertheless, Buddhism has very firm ethical roots based on the idea of a common human nature, and on the need to live an accountable life. Key elements include the necessity to overcome illusion and strip away selfish desire in order to find enlightenment. These are not requirements that depend on individual opinion and they are not relative to the situation or society a person comes from – they are regarded as the path to wisdom for *all people*. This places a very high demand upon the individual. It is a demand that is at least equal to those of other world religions but is achieved without apparent appeal to a transcendent 'Other'. Nevertheless, there are metaphysical claims that ground Buddhism. The authority for the demands it makes on individuals does not reside in 'God' but in the claim that becoming fully human is not something that can be achieved without application and that it is the only road to fulfilment and overcoming the emptiness of life.

The spiritual path and the becoming fully human are viewed by all world religions as two sides of one coin. It is in the unpacking of this claim into the formulation of ethical rules by different religions that variation occurs. The common ground between them is nevertheless more significant than the differences. This common ground, based on the idea of a single human nature, is often the poor relation in discourse concerning world religions but may well be where their true wisdom is to be found.

Living by rules

The fact that different religions claim different ethical rules seems to imply relativism. The relativist will claim that there is no way of unpacking in detail what it means to live an accountable life because every community has its own ideas. This position seems highly plausible as the rules of communities do, indeed, differ radically. Differences occur not only between religious, national or cultural environments but also between different branches of the same religion. As just one example, the position on sexual morality, IVF, contraception, homosexual relationships and divorce are radically different between Catholic and Protestant Christian groups, and even within the Protestant Churches.

There is no way of resolving these tensions as the groups have different starting points and appeal to different presuppositions. For instance:

- Protestant Christians will claim that the final revelation of God is given by Jesus and is recorded in the Bible. Most ethical dilemmas should be able to be resolved through careful study of the Bible or by God speaking directly to the individual in prayer and providing guidance for life.
- Catholic Christians will claim that Jesus came to found the Church and it is the Catholic Church which is the sole determinant of how life should be lived. For instance, Germain Grisez, one of the foremost and most conservative Catholic moral theologians, says: 'We believe that our Lord teaches in and through the Church and gives us the word of the Father. Hence, our submission to the Church's teaching is not submission to mere human opinions, but to the very word of God.'*

---

* *The Way of the Lord Jesus: Christian Moral Principles* (Quincy, Illinois, Franciscan Press, 1993), p. 570.

However, these positions, as stated, are close to caricatures and the actual positions are far more complex and subtle than such brief summary statements can express. Few Protestants seriously consider that the Bible has all the answers to modern life and certainly would acknowledge that it needs interpretation. Most would acknowledge that there is a wide spectrum of views within Christianity and that there is considerable debate about how issues such as genetics should be dealt with. Although the Catholic Magisterium speaks with a strong voice and insists that only it has the right to decide how lives should be lived and although in the last twenty years the freedom of discussion introduced by the Second Vatican Council has been radically restricted, nevertheless there is still a widespread diversity of views within Catholicism as to what it means to live a good life.

Almost all religious institutions wish to lay down rules as to how life should be lived and about what is right and what is wrong. They wish their people to be 'formed' in their faith tradition and to maintain a coherence of teaching in a world where increasing fragmentation of ideas is the norm. Postmodernism has contributed to this wish as many religious people have felt the need to retreat behind the fortress of their own certainties in order to withstand what they see as the tide of relativism. This has led to some religious groups becoming less tolerant and more insistent on inculcating uniformity of beliefs, with conservative elements engaging in a critique of culture where 'critique' implies negativity. Thus, they retreat into a fortress mentality. The institution then becomes increasingly important as it attempts to impose its own views on the individual churches, priests and places of worship which they control. From a sociological perspective, this is an understandable development. However, once religion becomes institutionalised, something precious and central can be lost. The whole idea of individual accountability to God is easily undermined and conformity to the group can become central.

Instead of a life of radical accountability to a transcendent Other, accountability to the rules of one's institution or community can easily become the supreme value. This opens the door to institutional evil to which religious institutions, as much as any other, are subject. The power of the institution is used to ensure conformity and compliance and no space remains for appeal beyond the mores of the institution as there is no conceptual space available for such an appeal. If the institution lays sole claim to determine the will of God or what it is to live an accountable life, then there is no ability to challenge and possibly reject the institution when it goes astray.

There is no institution, religious or otherwise, that has not made many errors and that has not used power to ensure compliance in ways that have left notions of truth and justice as victims. Religious institutions, indeed, have often been the chief enemies of the idea of a life of radical, individual accountability. Many religious people recognise precisely this. The head of the Catholic Congregation for the Doctrine of the Faith has emerged as one of the most conservative and reactionary forces in the present Church. Before he reached his present tremendously powerful position he recognised the point being made here and said:

> Since Newman and Kierkegaard, conscience has occupied with new urgency the centre of Christian anthropology. The work of both also represented, in an unprecedented way, the discovery of the individual who is called directly by God and who, in a world which scarcely makes God known any more, is able to become directly certain of God through the voice of conscience ... Over the Pope as the expression of the binding claim of ecclesiastical authority, there still stands one's own conscience, which must be obeyed before all else, if necessary, even against the requirement of ecclesiastical authority. This emphasis on the individual, whose conscience confronts him with a supreme and ultimate tribunal, and one which in the last resort is beyond the claim of external social groups, even the official Church ... also establishes a principle in opposition to increasing totalitarianism. Genuine ecclesiastical obedience is distinguished from any totalitarian claim which cannot accept any ultimate obligation of this kind beyond the reach of its dominating will.[*]

---

[*] Cardinal Ratzinger quoted in Herbert Vorgrimmler's *Commentary on the Documents of Vatican II*, p. 134.

This is well put and is entirely consistent with the argument of this book. Any good institution, in contrast to one intent on using power to impose its will, needs to recognise the truth of this statement. Note the wording: 'This emphasis on the individual, whose conscience confronts him with a supreme and ultimate tribunal, and one which in the last resort is beyond the claim of external social groups, even the official Church ...' This is precisely why an accountable life as envisaged in this chapter is not the same as an ethical life lived by the rules of an institution or by the rules of any religious group. In the case of a people who centre their life on following the ethical rules of a Church, they are effectively centring their life on a social group, even if this is a religious institution. Under no circumstances should such a group be the final focus of accountability. Cardinal Ratzinger's statement makes clear that accountability goes beyond any group to a direct call by God which can, in principle, contradict even the teaching of an individual's Church.

Conscience

Appeal to conscience raises the very real problem of how such claims can be assessed. Without a proper means of assessment talk of conscience can come very close to talk of personal inclination which can vary dependent on culture, situation and personal circumstance. Many terrible acts have been carried out by people who have claimed to be acting according to their conscience. Albert Schweitzer describes the quiet conscience as an invention of the devil as it is can be a way of imposing a person's own certainties on others or, alternatively, of individuals feeling virtuous because they have not infringed their own perception of ethical rules even though they may have ignored the demands of those around them.

If an accountable life is not to consist merely in:
- accountability to self (in which case self is the final arbiter) or
- accountability to the community or organisation of which a person forms part (in which case there is no possibility of appeal beyond the teaching and values of the community or organisation)

then the idea of accountability to some Absolute or Other is essential and this is a central part of an understanding of conscience. Conscience is a universal experience which can be nurtured or almost completely destroyed. It rests in the feeling that whenever a choice is made the individual is in some way accountable for that choice. Conscience is a process that does not depend simply on an intuition as to what an individual may at any given moment think is right. Conscience can be informed or not; it can be developed, or not. Conscience is not an infallible guide to truth and knowledge but it does exist as a faculty in each person. As Cardinal Ratzinger argued, it can mean that individuals are ultimately accountable for themselves to a higher authority than self or community.

By entering into the complexity of life – not being content to side simply with the decisions of state or Church or friends or family – conscience is nurtured. Conscience can be crushed and silenced by repeated refusals to engage in life as a complex experience, or by the refusal to engage seriously with other points of view. A developed conscience will stand in the shoes of fellow human beings, laugh with them, cry with them and share their humanity with them as an equal participant in the complexity of this mortal coil. The life lived purely by the rules may be acceptable to the community – whether a religious community or a secular community – but it is actually a refusal to engage meaningfully with the creative work of becoming fully human, which demands far more from an individual than this.

It is hard to measure or delineate what an accountable life of this sort might be like. It is far easier to talk of accountability to a set of rules laid-down by a state, organisation or religious institution (in other words accountability to ethics). If accountability is simply to ethics then there can be clear guidelines, and what it means to transgress the laid-down moral rules is unambiguous. The idea of accountability to some transcendent Absolute raises the very real question of how it is possible to know whether a person is acting according to a well-informed good conscience or according to an ill-informed conscience that is in some way deceived. It is a simple matter for someone to perform despicable acts and then to claim that 'God or conscience told me to do them'. Peter Sutcliffe who murdered prostitutes in a graveyard said that God told him to do it and what is more he is reported to have prayed before killing individual woman to determine whether his proposed victim was one that deserved death. The advantages, therefore, of claiming that a good life is an ethical life are very real as they avoid the danger of people who are mad or self-obsessed claiming that they acted according to their conscience and that their actions were thereby 'good'.

How is a good conscience to be judged? This book is arguing that conscience is not to be judged by accepted 'rules', but by what, then, is it to be judged? Martin Luther King said:

> Cowardice asks the question, 'Is it safe?' Expediency asks the question, 'Is it polite?' Vanity asks the question, 'Is it popular?' But conscience asks the question, 'Is it right?' And there comes a point when one must take a position that is neither safe, nor polite, nor popular, but one must take it because one's conscience tells him or her that it is right.

When Martin Luther King and other great figures talk of what is 'right', they do not mean this in a relative sense. They are rather expressing their conviction that there is a transcendent order that governs the universe that is not merely dependent on culture or accepted norms for ethical behaviour. They also share the conviction that there is a common human nature and living to fulfil this nature and to enable others to fulfil it, if they choose to do so, is significant and matters. It is a position grounded in the idea of individual accountability for the way in which each individual lives. Peter Sutcliffe had not considered the common humanity which he shared with his victims. He had not engaged with the complexity of issues that drives women to become prostitutes. He had not developed empathy to help him consider what it would be like to be a prostitute. He had not stood in their shoes and considered that they might need help and support rather more than his murderous hands. His conscience was, by all the standards of what it is to be human, incredibly ill formed.

It is this understanding that makes it possible to challenge and resist fundamentalism. Fundamentalists are not seeking to

respect the autonomy of others. They are not working to help others to have the freedom to fulfil their own human potential. Instead, they are imposing their own certainties on others with little recognition that they could be wrong about these certainties. It is one thing to stake one's own life on religious or moral certainties, but the possibility of being in error always exists and, therefore, to impose these certainties on others without their free choice is a position that needs to be challenged and rejected.*
Unless individuals are acting so as to foster their own and others' search for wisdom, compassion and insight based on the common human nature that all share, it is likely that their position will be flawed and will need to be challenged on at least some occasions.

Once it is accepted that all human beings share a common human nature and potential, then the task of each individual is to develop this potential but also to help others to develop their individual potentialities. This means that it can never be right to treat others as a means to an end or to mistreat others, whether physically or mentally, as any such treatment risks diminishing them rather than enabling them to fulfil their potential.

A life lived engaging with humanity, engaging with complexity, at a personal level engaging with decision making because the individual is accountable, faces two opposed challenges:

1. On the one hand this form of life allows for the possibility of the rejection of any set of ethical rules laid down by family, community, nation or institution because of the actual or perceived demand of a transcendent Absolute. In other words the moral rules accepted by any community may be rejected by an individual because of a responsibility to act in a way which these moral rules may consider unacceptable but which an individual feels called to carry out because of a higher demand:
   • Francis of Assisi responded to such a demand when he

---

* *What is Truth* by Peter Vardy (Alresford, John Hunt Publishing, 2003) explores the issue of what it means to talk of truth and why both postmodernism and fundamentalism are flawed positions.

rejected his parents outside the cathedral in Assisi in order to pursue what he saw as a call to a life of radical poverty and service;

- Luther responded to such a demand when he stood against the might of the established Church of his time and rejected central parts of its teaching which could easily have led to his death;

- Bonhoeffer responded to such a demand when he took part in a plot to assassinate Hitler even though murdering another human being is universally considered to be a wrong act. He was arrested and went to his death calmly assured that his absolute duty to act as he did was justified by the absolute responsibility he had;

- Gandhi responded to such a demand when, alone, he stood against the power of the British empire and the values it accepted and, as a result, was mocked, imprisoned and rejected by those in power;

- Nelson Mandela responded to such a demand when he rejected the moral rules of his society and paid the price of a prolonged gaol sentence;

- Vaclav Havel responded to such a demand when he continued to write and to publish poetry and plays which rejected the values of the communist government in his country and was sentence to four years in gaol.

- In Myanmar, Aung San Suu Kyi responded to such a demand when she stood by her calls for freedom and democracy in her country in spite of threats and violence against her and in spite of a culture where to do so invited the death penalty or, in her case, long years of house arrest.

Today it is easy to look back and admire such individuals but, at the time, they were figures of derision and their stands made sense only because they could appeal beyond the frontiers of the morality of their community to a higher duty to which they held themselves accountable.

2. On the other hand, there may be no clear way of measuring these actions by any clear ethical standard since they precisely go against the agreed ethical standards of their society. At the time, the commonly accepted morality accepted by the com-

munities in which these people lived would have rejected their actions and most of their fellow human beings would have been content to accept and live by the community rules. The refusal of these individuals to conform may, in retrospect, be praised but many unknown individuals take the same stand and are never recognised – they are rejected by their communities and are forced to live lives of exclusion from them sustained only by their commitment to an Absolute which not everyone would understand or accept. Some of them, of course, may be mistaken or deluded which is precisely where the problem arises. Once the certainty provided by ethical rules is abandoned, then the individual enters uncharted waters where there may be no clear markers and where the possibility of being in error can be very real.

These two positions are in tension and it is a tension which is not easily resolved. On the one hand are the heroes who centre their lives on an absolute demand which may call them beyond the frontiers of their existing community in obedience to some absolute duty and which may (or may not) lead to them one day being recognised for what they did. On the other hand, are similar individuals who transgress the ethical bounds of their community and could be mistaken or deluded. However, if their stand is based on what it is to be fully human and if their actions are designed to respect and foster the common humanity of others, then the scope for error may be limited.

An Austrian peasant who could not read or write provides a good example of an accountable life as here described. Franz Jagerstater owned a small farm and was married with four children when the Germans invaded Austria at the beginning of the Second World War. The invasion was widely popular in Austria and many people supported the Nazis. Jagerstater rejected them utterly. He was required to sell his crops through a local Nazi-owned co-operative but he refused to do so as this would have meant co-operating with evil-doers. Then a call went out that everyone of military age was required to join the army, Jagerstater refused to go. His friends told him that he had to go and the mayor of the local town came out to try and persuade him, saying that if he did not go he would be put to death. Still he refused. His wife pleaded with him saying that he had a duty to his family and his children and there was no point to the stand he was making. The mayor said that if he would volunteer to work in the local hospital he would be exempted from service and would therefore be safe. Still he refused – he considered that to compromise would be to give in to evil and he rejected this. He felt a duty to something absolute which went beyond any ethical duty and this was something that his friends and family were unable to understand. Jagerstater was duly killed and almost forgotten. His action seemed to have no point and no significance, yet today, sixty years later, his integrity and bravery are remembered long after all those who collaborated are forgotten. Yet it is not whether he is remembered or whether he is forgotten that is significant – many more died making similar stands against the Nazis – what is important is that he lived an accountable life. His conscience was informed of what it would mean to go with the flow of Nazi imperialism and such compliance would have been a denial of his humanity. He would not have been able to live with the knowledge that he was siding with evil, so accountable did he feel for his decision. The accountability he felt to a higher authority superceded accountability to his wife, his family, his community and even to himself. If more individuals had had the informed developed conscience of this man, the events of the Holocaust might well have been avoided.

Individualism and community

The great danger of this approach is that it appears to emphasise individuality at the price of community. If this were, indeed, the case then it would be a real criticism. This emphasis, however, is more apparent than real. Everyone lives in community and relationships are vital to forming and sustaining individuals. Human beings do not function well when isolated from each other but need to be in relationship with family, friends, neighbours and colleagues. Pursuing the common good which builds up the communities of which individuals form part is obviously essential to any human life. The issue is, however, whether such community relationships can be the final determinant of what it is to be fully human. Those who favour a life centred on ethics will answer 'yes' but it is the argument of this book that, however important community and relationships may be, they are not the final determinant of a human life: they do not by themselves enable a person to become fully what they are capable of being.

All human beings die essentially alone even if, physically, someone may be with them. This is part of the inescapable nature of the human condition that a material or scientific approach to humanity obscures. Today in the West most people insulate themselves from death and do not want to consider it or to talk about it, yet everyone has to die. In death every person is an individual, stripped of those relationships, possessions and reputations which in life seemed to mean so much. In Tolstoy's short story *The Death of Ivan Ilych* the story is told of a successful judge, Ivan, who lived a totally conventional life which he only began to question as he was dying. In the final weeks when he is in great pain and the doctors have admitted their inability to help him, he is left in his bed and has to wrestle with his pain alone. He also, for the first time, begins to look back over his life and wonders about how he has lived. During this time, he hears an inner voice speaking to him:

'What is it you want?' was the first clear conception capable of expression in words, that he heard.

'What do you want? What do you want?' he repeated to himself.

'What do I want? To live and not to suffer,' he answered.

And again he listened with such concentrated attention that even his pain did not distract him.

'To live? How?' asked his inner voice.

'Why, to live as I used to – well and pleasantly.'

'As you lived before, well and pleasantly?' the voice repeated.

Ivan comes to realise that 'living pleasantly' is an empty existence but it takes the process of dying to realise this. He has lived accountable to his community; he is accepted and considered respectable by his social circle and his associates in the legal profession. His family life is 'comme il faut' but his dying reveals the emptiness of his life. A short time before his death his wife comes in but by this time he has grown in wisdom. He recognises that his life was based on a mistake. He says, 'This is wrong, it is not as it should be. All you have lived for and still live for is falsehood and deception, hiding life and death from you.' As soon as he has admitted this thought, his hatred and his agonizing physical suffering again spring up, and with this suffering a consciousness of the unavoidable, approaching end. And to this is added a new sensation of 'grinding shooting pain and a feeling of suffocation.'

It is only in Ivan's dying moments that he finds hope and, in a sense, it is only in his dying that he lives for the first time. He lived dying and he died living. As Tolstoy put it: 'Ivan Ilych's life had been most simple and most ordinary and therefore most terrible.' It was terrible because he had never reflected on his life, he had never tried to develop a self, he had never been accountable. He was a good example of a drunk asleep in the cart of life pulled this way and that by unknown impulses of which he was not even aware.

Human beings tend to want to cluster together in a group for reassurance that their lives have purpose and they find confirmation that they are right and that their lives have meaning by conforming to the communities in which they live:

> Men feel their weakness, and to numbers run
> Themselves to strengthen, or themselves to shun;
> But though to this our weakness may be prone,
> Let's learn to live, for we must die alone.[*]

It is sometimes only in death that social cohesion is seen as a mask and the individual wakes up to the fact that he or she is an individual. It is only by living accountable to an ultimate Other that a person can deal with death, despair and the challenge of meaninglessness these bring. It is sometimes only when one is dying (and perhaps not even then) that one can ask oneself

---

[*] George Grabbe, 'The Borough', from *Clubs and Social Meetings*, 1810.

honestly whether one has lived a 'true' life, a life for which one would not be ashamed to render account. It is only when death comes near that the trappings of the world are stripped away and money, possessions, position and reputation count for nothing at all. It is then that a person may have to measure his or her life by other criteria.

This opens the door to two levels of ethical discussion based on two generally accepted but apparently contradictory intuitions:

1. That morality is not simply a construct: there are some absolutes. Purposeless cruelty to others, wanton destruction, torture or using human beings as a mere means to an end are absolutely wrong because they go against what it is to be human.
2. That there is no single valid moral system: some moral rules are contextual and based on the society in which individuals live and the institutions to which they belong.

This apparent tension can be resolved by recognising that they are two layers of morality:

1. **a meta-morality** which is absolute and which represents an absolute sense of individual accountability. This is grounded in actions which foster the development of individuals, enabling them to achieve their potential as human beings and to help others to do the same;
2. **a social morality** which is relative to the community, culture or institutions to which a person belongs.

The social morality may well contribute to an understanding of the meta-morality, but the meta-morality can never be wholly cashed in terms of the social morality. There will always be a tension between the two and, if the existence of the former is denied, then the power of the institution and community to impose the latter will be supreme and institutional evil will result. There is no way of being sure which social morality best fosters fulfilment of human potential and it seems likely, given the lessons of history, that this may develop over time.

Xenophanes of Kolophon, who was born about 580 BCE, was

one of the first of the great pre-Socratic philosophers and had a significant influence on those who came after him. He argued that God was one and unmoved (very different from the highly anthropomorphic pictures of the gods of his time). He wrote the following:

> The gods did not reveal, from the beginning,
> All things to us; but in the course of time,
> Through seeking we may learn, and know things better.
>
> But as for certain truth, no man has known it,
> Nor will he know it; neither of the gods,
> Nor yet of the things of which I speak.
>
> And even if by chance he were to utter
> The final truth, he would himself not know it;
> For all is but a woven web of guesses.[*]

This might be said of the relative moralities of our societies today – except that we have, under the guidance of Xenophanes' successor Aristotle, advanced further in our thinking. In Xenophanes' view, human beings could only guess at how life should be lived but he did recognise that, through seeking, we could come to have a better understanding. It was Aristotle who showed that human beings do not need to rely on guesswork but, through a careful examination of what it is to be human, can come to a closer understanding of what a fulfilled human life should be like. It is this that this book has attempted. We are still a long way from being clear on what it is to be fully human, but as our understanding of psychology, physiology, sociology, philosophy and theology deepens it may be possible to come to a much fuller and richer understanding of human potential than even that to which Aristotle aspired. In the meantime it is essential to recognise that our attempts at truth claims in this area will be at best approximations.

In the Christian tradition, Jesus said that he was the Truth and

---

[*] I was introduced to this quotation by Dr Catherine Cowley, my colleague at Heythrop College, University of London.

that the Truth would make human beings free. Obedience solely to the authority found within a community (be this nation, institution or Church) is a denial of the autonomy of individual human beings as moral agents. This does not mean, of course, that the individual should not listen to the accumulated wisdom and experience of the great traditions which have formed his or her thinking but, in the final analysis, this tradition can always be subject to challenge by a higher accountability to the Absolute.

If individuals are to act morally they need to be educated; they have to be helped to exercise a sense of responsibility for a life that is accountable not just to themselves or to the communities in which they live or the institutions to which they belong but to a transcendent Absolute. This is hard for communities and institutions to acknowledge. They would prefer their own understanding of ethics to be accepted as the ultimate without any challenge being raised. In the case of many religious institutions, they have the added advantage of being able to claim that they alone can mediate and reveal what an accountable life should be and, therefore, they can tend to substitute accountability to the institution for accountability to the Absolute. This, however, is an error. Whatever the strength of their claims, they cannot take away the possibility of an appeal by the individual beyond the morality of the institution to a higher imperative.

If it is accepted that there is some meta-morality provided by a sense of ultimate accountability and fulfilment of human nature, then bringing people to freedom and to a sense of responsibility is intimately connected with this ultimate. Socrates recognised this when he challenged the accepted culture of his society – he was condemned to death on the twin charges of atheism (as he did not believe in the state gods) and corrupting the young. He was held to have corrupted the young people who listened to him by enabling them to think for themselves and not simply to accept the values of their elders. The respectable citizens of Athens found this too uncomfortable and condemned Socrates to death. Similarly, many in today's modern institutions would find the idea of bringing people to individual freedom too challenging and unacceptable. As Carl Sagan says:

> All of us cherish our beliefs. They are, to a degree, self-defining. When someone comes along who challenges our belief system as insufficiently well-based – or who, like Socrates, merely asks embarrassing questions that we haven't thought of, or demonstrates that we've swept key underlying assumptions under the rug – it becomes much more than a search for knowledge. It feels like a personal assault.*

Each individual has to be responsible to the Absolute for every word, thought or action. The essence of religion should be the claim that there is a transcendent purpose for every individual grounded in their common humanity and a transcendent ground for their individual, free decisions. They are not just responsible to themselves; they are responsible to God or the ultimate ground of their being for becoming fully human. Martin Luther described this as living *coram deo*, before God, and recognised that it was an exceptionally hard task. Søren Kierkegaard said that such a life involved being 'suspended over 70,000 fathoms' outside the final authority and security of the community and with the ever-present possibility that a person's discernment of what is right might be mistaken.

The real problem is how this responsibility is to be worked out. It *cannot* be worked out by adherence to a set of ethical rules imposed by the community or religious group to which a person happens to belong, even if this organisation claims to speak with divine authority. Such an approach, as Cardinal Ratzinger recognised, denies individual autonomy and the search for Truth. This, then, creates the potential for a conflict between the individual and community.

Postmodernism is right that many truth claims in ethics are contextual but it is wrong to deny any absolute morality. This absolute still exists, grounded as Aristotle recognised, in what it

---

* Carl Sagan, *The Demon-haunted World* (London, Headline, 1996).

is to be human. Different ethical systems may conflict but they may nevertheless still contribute to the meta-morality as they may provide different pathways to the same end of becoming fully human. This can overcome the apparent tension between ethical rules within different communities. There is no doubt that different communities have evolved very different rules, but these different rules may still contribute to being human. For instance, in Islam a man is allowed four wives *but* only on condition that every wife must be treated completely equally and can be properly financially supported. Because of this, few men have more than one wife. Underneath, therefore, the social morality is a meta-morality which respects the dignity of each wife and demands that this be taken seriously. Similarly, the ethical rules developed by nomadic indigenous peoples to cope with their lifestyle are very different from those developed by settled, agricultural communities, but both can contribute to individuals within these communities fulfilling their potential (and, of course, both sets of rules can also become oppressive and can deny this possibility).

Individuals need to respect the ethical rules of the community within which they live, together with the tradition and wisdom from the past that has shaped and created these rules. This is what it means for a person to inform their conscience. It requires individuals to listen to the wisdom of the tradition in which they are formed and to seek to understand what has led to the views currently accepted in this community. However, having informed their conscience and listened carefully to the arguments and opinions of those in authority, then each individual must be willing, if he or she considers it necessary, to stand against the accepted conventions in order to be responsible to the Absolute or God. What is more, any community or religious tradition should respect and listen to those who reject or question the accepted conventions. recognising that these conventions may be flawed.

After the events of September 11, there was an almost unquestioned acceptance in the United States that those who caused the deaths in New York deserved to be hunted down and condemned. US forces toppled the Taliban regime in Afghanistan and hundreds of suspected members of Al-Qaida were sent to Camp X-ray in Cuba. They were not tried, were allowed no legal representation and were kept in harsh conditions. A spokesman for President Bush said that they were being treated as Americans would want them to be treated. Few in the United States really made an effort to understand the anger and outrage against the United States and its allies in Israel which had led a group of clearly intelligent people to sacrifice their lives. Palestinians have been murdered, persecuted, evicted from their homes and farms by an Israeli government intent on expanding its territory by force beyond the area allotted to Israel at its formation and in clear contravention of UN resolutions. They have been supported in doing this by billions of US dollars and the latest military hardware. The issue of Muslim grievances against the West including Palestinian claims about the activities of the state of Israel, corruption in Arab countries due to the influence of capitalism, Western support of corrupt regimes in the region to foster their own interests, as well as the disregard by Western capitalism for the religious values of devout Muslims, is hardly ever addressed. This finally led some to feel that they had no recourse left except to express their anger by an act which, whilst appalling, could be seen as justified in their eyes and in the eyes of some of their community. They were then branded as terrorists and the full might of the US military was unleashed against any who supported them. This represented a failure to engage with complexity or even to listen seriously to an alternative viewpoint. Yet within the US those who raise such questions are often persecuted or shouted down as being 'un-American'.

The Catholic Church has similar difficulty in listening to those who argue for married priests, for women priests, or for greater involvement of the laity in church government, and seeks to suppress discussion of these and related issues in Catholic universities or schools. There are various ways in which this is done. In 1990, the Catholic Magisterium in Rome issued *Ex Corde Ecclesiae*, a document which sought to set clear limits to what can be taught in Catholic faculties. It requires individuals teaching in Catholic institutions to obtain a *mandatum*[*] in order to confirm that their teaching represents the orthodoxy required by the Magisterium and enables teachers who do not accept this orthodoxy to be removed. Once again, this represents a failure to let individuals grapple with the complexity of the issues.

In Islam, there remains a widespread rejection of anyone who questions the place or status of the Qu'ran or even suggests that it might be interpreted in the light of conditions in the modern world. These issues cannot be discussed in many quarters without the real possibility of death threats being made.

It is very easy for institutions to insist that they are right and that voices of dissent must be quashed but this rejects precisely the point for which Cardinal Ratzinger so cogently argued.

There has been much discussion in recent years on the whole topic of human rights – the constitutions of both France and the United States of America are based on declarations of human rights and the United Nations' Declaration of Human Rights is recognised by every country throughout the world. These declarations recognise the fundamental equality of all human beings but it is only if these rights are innate rather than conferred by society that they can be binding. If rights are conferred by particular governments, then the same governments can take them away from particular groups (as, for instance, happened in the United States when the human rights of Al-Qaida supporters were effectively taken away simply because of their membership of an organisation and without any trial or means of appeal). If, however, human rights are innate and are grounded in what it is to be human (as the US constitution proclaims), then the other

---

[*] On 15 June 2001 the Catholic Bishops of the United States drew up the following statement, to be signed by every Catholic teacher applying for a *mandatum*: 'I hereby declare my role and responsibility as a professor of a Catholic theological discipline within the full communion of the Church. As a professor of a Catholic theological discipline, therefore, I am committed to teach authentic Catholic doctrine and to refrain from putting forth as Catholic teaching anything contrary to the Church's magisterium.' This has raised issues of academic freedom within United States' universities which are still being discussed.

side of these rights is the issue of responsibilities, the responsibilities that every person has to other human beings because of the fundamental equality of all human beings. In religious terms this can be expressed by speaking of every individual as a 'child of God' or as unique and special before God. This recognition of fundamental equality represents the conviction of the three great theistic religions and also of Buddhism which is sometimes described as the religion of infinite compassion for every other human being – although Buddhists would not express this conviction in language about God.

Some religious people are very good at being sure that *they* are right and that others who do not share their moral views are wrong. This book is arguing that this view is mistaken and fails to take seriously the difference between the absolute meta-morality and different relative detailed moralities. These different detailed moralities may, as has been argued, enable human flourishing although equally, of course, they may prevent such flourishing. It is when families, communities or organisations become oppressive and use their power to stifle questioning or dissent, or when educational institutions discourage young people from coming to freedom and an individual sense of responsibility that institutional evil arises and this, perhaps more than anything else, deprives individuals of the possibility of fulfilling their potential.

What if there is no Absolute?

There will be those who reject any transcendent Absolute; there will be those who reject any common human nature; there will be those who affirm that life is meaningless and that human beings are merely a biological accident with the sole purpose of passing their genes onto the next generation. It is, of course, possible that they may be right and this may be true but, if so, it is a bleak picture, and one which few accept. The ideas of postmodernism and thinkers like Dawkins are actually shared by a tiny minority of the world's population – basically an educated elite based in Western universities who have created theories which they find convincing but which most others regard with incredulity. In spite of attacks on the irrelevance of religion, on its primitive nature and on it being a psychological prop for those who cannot face meaninglessness, the religious imperative is alive and well throughout the world and it remains the case that some of the most highly educated individuals in all cultures of the world have a deep religious sense and commitment. Of course, it is possible that they may all be naïve and deceived but given the calibre of these people it seems appropriate to take their claims seriously. Nevertheless it does, of course, remain possible that the critics are right and that those who say the world has meaning are deluded.

In C. S. Lewis' Narnia Chronicles, the Witch takes two of the children beneath the earth where they are hypnotised by an enchanted fire and led to believe that the Witch's kingdom is all that exists. She tells them that there is no sun and that the world of Narnia, which means so much to them, is just a make-believe story. They are nearly ready to believe her lies when one of their companions, Puddleglum, partially stamps out the Witch's hypnotic fire and says to her:

> "Suppose we have only dreamed, or made up all those things – trees and grass and sun and moon and Aslan himself. Suppose we have. Then all I can say is that, in that case, the made-up things seem a good deal more important than the real ones. Suppose this black pit of a kingdom is the only world. Well, it strikes me as a pretty poor one. And that's a funny thing, when you come to think of it. We're just babies making up a game, if you're right. But four babies playing a game can make a play world which licks your real world hollow. That's why I'm going to stand by the play-world. I'm on Aslan's side even if there isn't any Aslan to lead it. I'm going to live as like a Narnian as I can even if there isn't any Narnia."*

This is perceptive. It may only be by seeking wisdom and perspicuity, accountable to an Absolute Other, that meaning, hope and freedom from despair can be found – and this may be a part of what it is to be human. This may be true even if no such

---

* C. S. Lewis, *The Silver Chair* (London, HarperCollins, 1998), p. 145.

Absolute exists. It is the fundamental conviction of the great world religions that such an Absolute does exist and that responsibility to it is the key to a fulfilled, fully human life. This may be as true today as ever in the past. There is no proof, simply the wisdom and experience of many great human beings in every society down the centuries. For many, this may be enough – there may be nothing more.

Perhaps it is only those who invest their life in this way who will realise the reality of this Absolute. Another quotation from the Narnia Chronicles may make this clear:

"Oh Aslan," said she [Lucy], "it was kind of you to come."

"I have been here all the time," said he, "but you have just made me visible."

"Aslan," said Lucy almost a little reproachfully. "Don't make fun of me. As if anything *I* could do would make *you* visible!"

"It did," said Aslan. "Do you think I wouldn't obey my own rules?"[*]

Lucy did not create Aslan, but she made him visible. Similarly humans do not make truth, but it may only be in the pursuit of truth and in being open to its existence that truth may appear. The existence of a transcendent Absolute or the value of an accountable life may only be apparent to those who live such lives and they may be driven to this either by the meaningless-ness and despair found everywhere else or by the lure or attraction of beauty, of music and of a commitment to the idea of an absolute distinction between living a fulfilled life and failing to take human potential seriously. These are unfashionable ideas these days but they still have a power to persuade. In the Franciscan tradition, God is described as a lover who lures individuals towards God by the presence of beauty in the world and this idea is as relevant today as it was 800 years ago. However, in order to make a response to this, each individual must recognise the human condition for what it is and then make

---

[*] C. S. Lewis, *The Voyage of the Dawntreader* (London, HarperCollins, 1998), p. 123.

a genuine attempt to address the situation in which they find themselves.

Pascal recognised this in his famous and misunderstood 'wager' argument. He said:

> Your desired destination is faith but you do not know the road. You want to cure yourself of unbelief and you ask for remedies: learn from those who were hampered like you and who now wager all they possess. These are people who know the road you would like to follow; they are cured of the malady for which you seek the cure; so follow them and begin as they did – by acting as if they believed ... In the natural course of events this in itself will make you believe, this will tame you.[*]

The original French word for 'tame' means 'make like a beast' and has echoes of an animal being tamed. However, it is best translated as 'train' or 'form'. Embarking on the search for truth and living an accountable life may help the individual to come to recognise the truth of what is being claimed and see that beyond the dragon of despair there is hope and meaning.

The problem is that postmodernism has led us to lose confidence in the very idea of truth,[†] and as such its impact has been devastating. It has seduced a whole generation into thinking that the search for truth and wisdom and the attempt to live a fulfilled life are irrelevant and naïve ideas. It is time to reawaken confidence in the idea of a fulfilled human nature and in helping ourselves and each other to care for our selves by living fulfilled lives.

It is perhaps significant that postmodernism has moved on (as one would expect – it is not a static thing) and, ironically, many writers who have been branded as postmodern now have a commitment to ideas such as the importance of justice as an absolute and valuing 'the Other' for who he or she really is. However, the epistemology of such claims is rarely examined – the easiest way, and perhaps the only way, of underpinning such

---

[*] Blaise Pascal, *Letter to Chanaut*, 15 June 1646.

[†] See *What is Truth* by Peter Vardy (Alresford, John Hunt Publishing, 2003).

claims lies in the affirmation of a transcendent Absolute but this, of course, is precisely what postmodernism has abandoned. However, the irony of this re-evaluation turns to near tragedy when one considers that a whole generation has had currency values in the area of faith, wisdom and truth undermined and destroyed.

A Way Forward

The Western world increasingly suffers from a perceived lack of meaning brought on by the so-called 'death of God' and the influence of postmodernism. Seeing human beings as a bio-logical accident without meaning or purpose has led to many of the difficulties at the heart of modern society. This has been accompanied by an ethical impotence because no intellectual framework seems to exist to challenge this meaninglessness. In spite of the speed of scientific advance, people have less and less time and throw themselves into increasing activity to disguise from themselves the true state they are in. Despair lurks behind many lives although individuals make every effort to avoid recognising this.

It has been the argument of this book that there is a way forward – a way grounded in the philosophy of Aristotle and the Natural Law tradition which concentrates on the importance of individuals fulfilling their potential. This has positive implica-tions for germ line and somatic cell genetic engineering as these seek to eliminate physical defects but it has even greater importance for the spiritual development of human beings. Concentration on the physical side of what it is to be human runs the very real risk that it is only the physical side that is valued and individuals come increasingly to be judged by their appear-ance or, in the future, by their genetic profile. All the great world religions take a stand against this and claim that there is a 'some-thing more' which represents by far the more important aspect of what it is to be human. Concentration on the physical side con-stantly neglects this aspect. Central to the 'something more' is the search for wisdom, perspicuity and insight (chapter eleven) and, particularly, the importance of each individual developing a self by reference to something Absolute that lies beyond family, community, nation or religious institution and which aids the development of other individuals to their full potential. Once this is accepted then it can never be right to hurt or diminish other human beings – the task is always to respect them as ends in themselves and to help them to realise their potential.

Institutions, particularly schools, universities and also religious institutions, need to take active steps in the following areas:

1. They need to encourage an understanding of what it means to live a fulfilled human life and to help individuals to comprehend that fulfilling human potential cannot be understood simply in physical or material terms. This will require the nurturing of the spiritual side of human nature and an appreciation of the importance of the search for absolute values. Many will be uncomfortable with this as it will challenge prevailing values accepted in society today. It will also challenge those who simply want to be comfortable and happy and see human fulfilment merely in these terms.

2. They need to develop a sense of personal responsibility in individuals so that, whilst appreciating the traditions from the past which have formed the communities of which they are a part, they nevertheless recognise a wider vision of accountability. Individuals then need to be helped and supported to take on board the demands that this accountability may make. This path will be difficult as in many cases is will not be clear what is right and discernment will be essential. Ethical dilemmas will need to be approached in fear and trembling because of their complexity. The approaches taken within different communities will be important guide posts, but that is all they are. In the end, each person has to be responsible for his or her own decisions and be willing to account for them not to self, not to community but to something ultimate which lies beyond all ethical difference. This can only be done by open and frank debate and certainly not by simply attempting to inculcate young people into the certainties of their elders.

3. They need to be prepared to listen when the norms and rules of the institution are challenged. This is exceptionally hard

and few institutions are willing to do this but it is only in so doing that institutional evil, which is built into the very structures of the societies in which human beings live, can be challenged.

Philosophy needs to stop playing intellectual games and emphasising reason alone. Philosophy, if it is to be of service to humanity, needs to be about a search for wisdom and, as soon as this is forgotten, then it becomes an impoverished and futile exercise which may be a good way of passing the time or even a way of gaining promotion in philosophy departments of Western universities but little else. Philosophy needs to address the human condition and to help people to find a way forward – to do this it needs to come out of its self-imposed ghetto and work closely with psychology, sociology, anthropology, theology and the natural sciences to seek to understand more fully what it is to live a human life.

As individuals we each have to care for our selves, we each have to take responsibility for our lives and for the self that we choose to construct. If we choose not to think and to occupy our lives with trivialities, then these trivialities will eventually pale and will come to seem like empty vanities. If we choose to create ourselves in our own image then that is our choice, but it will end in despair. If we choose to create ourselves in the image of our community then this, also, will end in despair as we eventually come to recognise that this framework is a social construct which cannot provide meaning. Nevertheless, this book has argued that there is a way forward.

There is no proof that life is not meaningless. There is no proof that human beings have a common human nature. There is no proof that human potential extends beyond the physical and that there is a spiritual side of human beings that is more important than any amount of genetic engineering. There is no proof that there is any transcendent Other. However, lack of proof is not the same as lack of truth. Some will stake their lives on this truth. They will put self in second place and will gladly live in and conform to their community but, in the final analysis, they will be willing to stand for what is true and what is just even against their own community. They will seek to live accountable lives. Such people claim to have found a meaning, a purpose and a wisdom that transcends the physical, the trivial and the self. The choice is simple – either such people have fulfilled their potential as human beings and this is something to which we can all aspire or they have lived their lives in folly and in ignorance.